D1649161

*a* SAVOR THE SOUTH™ *cookbook*

# Tomatoes

SAVOR THE SOUTH™ *cookbooks*

*Tomatoes,* by Miriam Rubin (2013)
*Peaches,* by Kelly Alexander (2013)
*Pecans,* by Kathleen Purvis (2012)
*Buttermilk,* by Debbie Moose (2012)

*For David, who gave me a garden*

# Contents

*a* SAVOR THE SOUTH™ *cookbook*

# Tomatoes

# Introduction

hey come in all shapes, sizes, and colors, from pink to peachy, from green to tangerine, from brick red to chocolaty-purple. They're sun-kissed, vine-ripened, with skins so thin they can barely contain the juice. Some are intensely sweet; others have tart undertones. The tomatoes of summer—I adore them all.

Tomatoes are the most widely grown vegetable in home gardens. The hottest thing going at farmers' markets. The most anticipated offering in community-supported agriculture baskets. Each season brings more types and wilder colors, and tomatoes become ever more appreciated. Did anyone ever write a song about radishes or kale? I don't think so.

Chances are if you're picking up this book, you already love tomatoes. You're already humming the song.

Tomatoes have long been a staple of southern gardens and cooking. Food writer John Egerton called them "the sun-ripened sirens of summer." Each part of the season has its amazing tomato moments. The first taste. The second slice. The day the big heirlooms arrive at the farmers' market, with everyone squinting in the sun and smiling wide. Lugging away full baskets of tomatoes purchased from tired, proud farmers. Don't forget the little tomatoes, the cherries and the pears, sassy-sweet nuggets of flavor.

Never fear, this book will be useful year-round because tomatoes are available year-round. And the bad old cardboard supermarket tomato, shipped green, gassed with ethylene so it "pinks up," is easier than ever to avoid. Because we began to pay attention to taste and demanded quality, many supermarkets carry an ever-expanding selection of flavorful tomatoes in all shapes and colors. And there are always good-quality canned tomatoes. For some recipes in this book, canned tomatoes are best. Or second best. And I have highlighted the recipes that bring out the most flavor in less-than-perfect tomatoes. Of course, nothing beats fresh tomatoes in season, especially locally grown. Especially grown close to home.

In my garden, I grow many vegetables that I love, from beets to peppers to potatoes to cucumbers, with all sorts of stuff in between the rows, but I'll admit to a tomato bias. "How are your tomatoes doing?" I ask fellow growers, because the answer is so often the measure of the garden itself.

We have friends who time their yearly visit to coincide with the ripening of the Brandywines. We throw an annual party for my food-writer colleagues at the height of the tomato harvest. Everyone, except for those who grow their own, leaves here with a basketful. Some of my friends prefer to visit at the close of the season, when I'm frying and pickling the green tomatoes.

While I look at food with a gardener's eye, I also see it through the eyes of a chef. My days are busy planning meals and planting plots, both strong passions, although I've been cooking food longer than I've been nurturing a garden. I watched my mother tend her garden, and she observed her own mother. My mother is still growing flowers and vegetables, and we chat frequently about gardens, each of us gloating some, as my vegetables ripen three weeks ahead of hers but her flowers are prettier. Early on, together, we canned her homegrown tomatoes in home-brewed tomato juice, adding a sprig of basil to each jar. My love of tomatoes was precocious.

## In the South

In this book, I'm looking at tomatoes through the lens of the South, where they're an important element in so many dishes. As cookbook author Virginia Willis writes, "Tomatoes are a key ingredient in both traditional and new Southern cooking." After all, the South is the region of the United States where tomatoes were first introduced and accepted—once people believed they weren't poisonous.

"They thrive in the South," writes Willis. "They love the blistering heat and the fertile soil. Tomatoes may only grow in the summer months, but in the South, they are enjoyed year-round."

In this region, with its lovely, long growing season—some areas enjoying two harvests, early and late—a plate of tomatoes is not only welcome but *expected* on the table at every meal. When it's too steamy to turn on the stove, you can turn to a tomato sandwich, nearly a food group in itself. Once the juicy slicers ripen, people just grab the soft white bread, a knife, and the mayo, opening things up for endless passionate discourse on which mayo to use—homemade or store-bought, Duke's or Hellmann's.

Homes and restaurants all over the South show off tomatoes with pride, bragging on their gardens and growers. Heirloom tomato salads appear everywhere, some fancy, some more basic, sometimes just the perfect refreshing combination of tomatoes, cucumbers, and onions. Honestly, in the heat of tomato season, nothing is better than a platter of multicolored tomatoes in their prime, freshly sliced, drizzled with fruity olive oil, with maybe a drop of mild vinegar, perhaps a few slices of Vidalia onion, and plenty of salt and black pepper. Except, of course, plucking sun-warmed cherry tomatoes right from the vine. You can do a lot to tomatoes, or you can let them shine in all their juicy glory.

## In the Kitchen

In the South, when the days get a touch cooler, tomatoes are enjoyed stewed, cobblered, and baked under a mantle of crumbs. Big skillets of simmering tomato gravy are ladled over split biscuits or sliced tomatoes. Tomatoes are stirred into soups, hot or cold, creamy or chunky, mild or spicy. Red and green tomatoes are baked in pies, sweet or savory.

Near the end of the season, there's the rush to put up the harvest, to make sauce, jam, chutney, pickles, signature ketchup, chow-chow, and sweet-and-spicy spreads, keeping tomatoes on the table all year-round. And as frost threatens, green tomatoes are breaded with flour, cracker crumbs, or cornmeal and fried in bacon drippings, then served with eggs and bacon, country ham, pimento cheese, buttermilk–black pepper dressing, or a sweet-tart tomato conserve. Writes cookbook author Sheri Castle: "There's nothing like a tomato to perk things up."

## At the Fair

Tomatoes are celebrated and feted throughout the South, where festivals crown tomato queens and their juniors, tommy-toes. There are tomato-throwing contests, tomato recipe contests, and tomato-eating contests. At the Lauderdale Tomato Festival in 2007 in Ripley, Tennessee, young and old volunteers helped build the World's Largest 'Mater Sandwich. Atlanta hosts the Attack of the Killer Tomato Festival, where chefs and mixologists are paired with farmers to create a new dish or tomato libation.

Other festivals pay homage to particular tomatoes or tomatoes grown within a certain region, where soil and water—the *terroir*—produce superior fruit. A short list includes the Hanover Tomato Festival in Virginia, the Grainger County Tomato Festival in Tennessee, the Bradley County Pink Tomato Festival in Arkansas, and the French Market Creole Tomato Festival in New Orleans.

More serious but still fun are tomato tastings where dedicated home-growers, farmers, and tomato enthusiasts gather to learn about new or newly discovered varieties and compare tasting notes and growing information. Each year, there are more types of tomatoes to taste and celebrate.

The *Winston-Salem Journal* has held a tomato tasting at the beginning of August for about ten years. The food editor, Michael Hastings, has observed the number of tomato varieties exploding during this time. At the 2011 tasting, there were ninety different types to sample.

"It's very unscientific, but people get a kick out of trying new varieties," he said. "They're invited to taste and give feedback. They use the tasting as a step toward deciding what to grow for the next year's crop." In 2011, the favorite was Mexico Midget, a small red cherry tomato. "It had an unusually complex flavor," Hastings said, "a lot of flavor in a small package."

The 2011 Tomatopalooza, a tomato tasting held outside of Raleigh, North Carolina, offered 166 tomatoes for sampling. Which tomato won? A bright tangerine cherry tomato called Sungold, developed by a Japanese seed company, that has been garnering devotees ever since it hit the scene in 1992. One commentator wrote that Sungolds are so good they should perhaps be eliminated from competition. Mexico Midget also placed in a four-way tie for the most unusual tomato.

The Carrboro, North Carolina, Farmers' Market has been hosting a Tomato Day for more than fifteen years. It started with about ten varieties of tomatoes, and it wasn't really a tasting then, more like a viewing, according to farmer and tomato grower Alex Hitt of Peregrine Farm. "The market is as much about consumer education as it is about selling tomatoes. Initially, we just wanted to expose customers to different tomatoes other than the normal red hybrids."

Now the tasting features around eighty-three different types, which are cut up for sampling. They've figured out a way around the dilemma of Sungolds always winning: there's no voting for favorites. Prior to this, Sungolds always placed first, until they were put in a separate cherry tomato category. The market also encourages farmers to provide samples at their stalls or to offer some kind of tomato dish or recipe throughout tomato season.

## What's in an Heirloom?

While it seems there is an explosion of *new* tomatoes, "new" is perhaps a misnomer. Some older tomato varieties have been saved, others have been rediscovered, and some have been created. Not all are considered heirlooms. Heirloom tomatoes are old varieties, termed "heritage vegetables" by food historian William Woys Weaver. These tomatoes are grown from seeds that people saved and handed down through the generations. Heirloom tomatoes are open-pollinated, which means that their seeds, if saved, can be replanted the following year and the same type of tomato plant should grow, barring any mutations. Seeds that are saved from hybrid tomatoes (such as Big Boy or Early Girl) will not produce the same plant.

In Carolyn J. Male's gorgeous book, *100 Heirloom Tomatoes for the American Garden*, Male and fellow tomato expert Craig LeHoullier have divided heirloom tomatoes into categories. It gets a little technical. And for the most part, it doesn't matter much to tomato buyers or diners at restaurants or gardeners, except as a way of understanding the industry. Yet it does matter, because the word "heirloom" is on the verge of becoming so overused it loses its meaning. These are the categories:

*Family heirlooms*: Some of these seeds arrived with immigrants who grew the tomatoes in their home countries. These tomatoes are literally treasured heirlooms. Growing them in our gardens gives us a direct link to the tomato past.

*Commercial heirlooms*: These are tomatoes that seed companies introduced before 1940. Many of today's hybrids are related to these tomatoes.

*Created heirlooms*: Green Zebra—that crisp, sweet-tart, green-striped, delightful little tomato that chefs love—is a perfect example of a created heirloom. Basically, two heirlooms or an heirloom and a hybrid are crossed to create a new tomato, combining the best characteristics of both.

## In the Beginning

Tomatoes originated on a narrow strip of land on the western coast of South America, in the mountains of Chile and Peru. Then, somehow, this wild fruit migrated to the gulf coast of Central America, where it was cultivated. Tomatoes are the only species known that was not cultivated in the place it was discovered, according to Barbara Melera of D. Landreth Seed Company, the oldest seed house in the United States.

According to Andrew F. Smith in *The Tomato in America: Early History, Culture, and Cookery*, tomatoes were domesticated by the Mayans and other Mesoamerican peoples who used them in cooking. Tomatoes also were adopted and eaten by the Aztecs, who mixed them with chiles and pounded squash seeds for a type of salsa. Smith posits that perhaps tomatoes initially were accepted because they resembled what we know today as the tomatillo, or husk tomato, which is unrelated to the tomato but thought to have been native to Mexico.

Aztecs called this new plant *xitomatl*. After the tomato's discovery by the Spanish during the conquest of Mexico, which began in 1519, the name became *tomate*. According to Smith, "By the sixteenth century this fruit was cultivated at least in the southern part of Mexico."

## Tomatoes Begin Their Spread

"Beginning in the sixteenth century," writes Charles C. Mann in his book *1493: Uncovering the New World Columbus Created*, "Europeans carried tomatoes around the world. After convincing themselves that the strange fruits were not poisonous, farmers planted them from Africa to Asia."

Tomatoes arrived in Spain shortly after the Spanish Conquest and in Italy about twenty years later. "They were used for culinary purposes in Seville at least by 1608," writes Smith, "probably in salad with cucumbers." Tomatoes first appear in a cookbook in Naples, Italy, in 1692, in a recipe that translates as "Tomato Sauce Spanish-Style." The recipe combines parsley, onions, garlic, salt, pepper, oil, and vinegar with peeled tomatoes, according to Alan Davidson in *The Oxford Companion to Food*.

"In a small way," notes Charles Mann, "the [tomato] plant had a cultural impact everywhere it moved. Sometimes not so small— one can scarcely imagine southern Italy without tomato sauce."

## Tomatoes Were Not Always the Beloved Fruit

Tomatoes spread throughout the Mediterranean, where they became a presence in many dishes in Turkey, Greece, and North Africa and were especially popular in the cooking of Sephardic Jews. But in other parts of Europe, many still would not eat tomatoes. According to rabbi and food historian Gil Marks, northern Ashkenazi Jews also avoided the tomato and referred to it, in Yiddish, as *treyfene epl*, or unkosher apple. It was only later, after "acculturation" in America and Israel, that tomatoes gained acceptance.

Tomatoes are members of the nightshade family, which includes eggplants and potatoes but also the aptly named deadly nightshade, so tomatoes, too, were declared to be poisonous. Some early herbalists linked them to the mandrake plant, which was considered an aphrodisiac. In the Bible, the Hebrew word for mandrake was *dudaïm*, which translates as love apples. Another name for tomatoes was *mala insana*, which is Greek for unhealthy fruit. On a more positive note, the Italian name for them was *pomi d'oro*, which means golden apples, perhaps because these first tomatoes were gold in color.

Tomatoes were grown in English gardens in the late 1500s, but at that time, they were considered merely ornamental plants. The fruit was not consumed, though sometimes it served medicinal purposes. Tomatoes were said to have a "rank smell," which was "very strong and offensive," and the fruit was thought to be "dangerous." According to Smith, even though it was understood that Italians and Spaniards were eating tomatoes (and living!), these negative attitudes "prevailed in Britain and in the British North American colonies for over two hundred years."

Things do change. By the mid-1700s, some Britons were eating tomatoes. These included Jewish families, many of whom were of Spanish or Portuguese descent and had a tradition of enjoying tomatoes. And by the late eighteenth century, tomatoes were found to be "in daily use."

## Getting to America

Throughout the sixteenth century, tomatoes were not eaten in what is today the United States. People knew of them, and it is documented that in the late seventeenth century, tomatoes were grown in gardens in the Carolinas. However, it wasn't until the early to mid-1800s that people truly began to warm up to them. Tomatoes came here in various ways—from Spanish explorers, from British colonists, and in the pockets of Italian immigrants in the 1840s.

Smith writes, "Tomatoes may have also been introduced from the Caribbean." It is also possible that some forms of tomato cookery, especially as it arose from "the exuberant Creole cuisines of the islanders" (as Karen Hess noted in her commentaries on Mary Randolph's *The Virginia Housewife*), were brought to the South by enslaved African women, many of whom had traveled through the West Indies and became cooks in wealthy southern households both before and after emancipation.

The first known reference to tomatoes in a southern cookbook was in 1770, in *A Colonial Plantation Cookbook: The Receipt Book of Harriot Pinckney Horry*. Horry lived in Charleston, South Carolina, and the recipe was a method for preserving tomatoes, "To Keep Tomatoos for Winter use." By the close of that century, Smith says, South Carolinians were sending tomato seeds and cookery to other parts of the United States.

"Sources indicate that tomato cookery was well established in Southern states by the mid-eighteenth century," writes Smith in his other tomato book, *Souper Tomatoes: The Story of America's Favorite Food*. From the South, tomatoes slowly spread northward up the Atlantic coast and into the rural regions.

Seventeen tomato recipes appeared in Mary Randolph's cookbook, *The Virginia Housewife or Methodical Cook*, published in 1824. Randolph was Thomas Jefferson's cousin. Included in her book are two recipes for tomato marmalade, plus "Tomato Catsup," "Gaspacho—Spanish" (not terribly different from modern recipes), "Eggs and Tomatos," and "Tomato Soy" (which seems to be a hot sauce). Also there are recipes entitled "To Scollop Tomatos" and "To Stew Tomatos."

Tomato recipes are also found in *The Kentucky Housewife* by Mrs. Lettice Bryan, published in 1839. In this book, tomatoes are dressed raw, made into ketchup, stewed, baked, and broiled. There is also a recipe for ripe tomatoes, peeled and skinned, sliced, dipped in grated bread, and fried in butter until brown.

Another early cookbook, *Mrs. Hill's New Cook Book* by Annabella Hill, was published in 1867 with the subtitle, *Especially Adapted to the Southern States*. In it are recipes for a spicy green tomato sauce; a brined-tomato pickle made with "two-thirds ripe" tomatoes; "Ochra and Tomatoes"; tomato fritters prepared with "green corn," eggs, and flour and fried in lard; a tomato salad made with thinly sliced peeled tomatoes "season[ed] with salt, pepper, sugar, and a little onion, [and] very little vinegar"; and a tomato paste spiked with sugar, pepper, mace or nutmeg, and apple vinegar.

It is indisputable that many of these recipes sound similar to dishes we make today. Maybe some of the methods have changed and some ingredients have been updated, but it is obvious that southern tomato dishes have deep roots and a long, delicious history.

Southern tomato cookery had other important and spicy influences. Writes Smith in *The Tomato in America*: "In Louisiana, Creole, Spanish, Cajun, and French cuisines fused with Native American and African cooking practices to create a culinary caldron that influenced American cooking even before Louisiana was purchased from France by President Thomas Jefferson." He recounts that tomatoes were grown and consumed by French settlers in eighteenth-century New Orleans and were sold in markets there as early as 1812.

## Improving the Early Tomato

Thomas Jefferson first tasted tomatoes in Europe, and he sent seeds back from France in the early 1780s. According to notes from Monticello, his daughter left behind numerous tomato recipes, including ones for cayenne-spiked tomato soups, gumbo, and green tomato pickles. In 1806, tomatoes were purchased and served at presidential dinners. Beginning in 1809, Jefferson grew tomatoes in his garden at Monticello.

But those tomatoes, according to Barbara Melera, were not the delicious tomatoes we eat today. Early tomatoes were seedy and had little flesh, deep ribbing, and substantial seed pockets.

Tomato seeds were vended commercially at the beginning of the nineteenth century. In 1820, the D. Landreth Seed Company sold seeds for a yellow-fleshed sandwich-sized tomato that was deeply ribbed. As lovely as it sounds, it wasn't well accepted and was pulled after about three years. Instead, the company started selling a large red cherry tomato and a yellow pear tomato, which were eaten raw. These remained popular for the next twenty years. These little tomatoes are thought to be very close to the original wild tomatoes from South America.

While the red cherry tomato and yellow pear tomato were popular, bigger tomatoes still left something to be desired. According to Carolyn Male, farmers and gardeners worked hard on making tomatoes better, selecting seeds from the best fruits. "In this simple way, there was continuous improvement in available tomato varieties." As she notes, the heirlooms we so admire would not exist without this early selection by farmers.

One grower in particular helped develop the juicy, smooth-skinned tomato we love today. In the 1850s, Dr. Hand, a gentleman in Baltimore County, Maryland, crossbred a large, crumpled, convoluted tomato that had delicious flesh but bitter, thick skin with a watery, smooth, but tasteless tomato that had very thin skin. For more than twenty years, he grew these tomatoes, carefully selecting seeds from the best of each harvest in order to breed a stable fruit that he called the Trophy Tomato. It was lauded as an early, important advance in horticulture.

In 1870, Colonel George E. Waring Jr. of Newport, Rhode Island, purchased the Trophy Tomato seeds from Dr. Hand. He then sold individual seeds for 25 cents and ran a competition, offering $100 to the person who used them to grow the "heaviest tomato." In *Heirloom Vegetable Gardening: A Master Gardener's Guide to Planting, Seed Saving, and Cultural History*, William Woys Weaver writes that "this was one of the first tomato varieties to revolutionize tomato growing."

Trophy Tomatoes became a success, being widely distributed across the country and carried by nearly every major American seed company at the time. Writes Weaver, "Trophy initiated a long line of nineteenth century hybrids that have since become tomato classics."

## Southern Tomatoes

Is there an original southern tomato? There are certain heirloom tomatoes with southern provenance that grow well in the South. These have loyal followings and evocative, place-setting names, such as Georgia Streak, Ozark Pink, Pike County, Arkansas Traveler, Missouri Pink Love Apple, Royal Hillbilly, and Old Virginia. German Johnson, the beloved pink tomato, hails from Virginia and North Carolina. Newer tomatoes are being developed all the time to address the particular hot and humid conditions in the South.

Other tomato seeds came over from France or Italy or traveled here from Mexico, such as Zapotec, a ruffled pink tomato. Some varieties came from up north: Brandywine is from Pennsylvania, and Amish Paste hails from an Amish community in Wisconsin. Popular purple-fruited tomatoes were brought over from Russia and Siberia, including Purple Russian, Black from Tula, Black Krim, Black Prince, and Paul Robeson, which was named to honor the singer. Cherokee Purple, however, is from Tennessee, and it is believed to have been grown by the Cherokee Indians.

So if you're thumbing through a seed catalog, thinking about what to plant in the South, choose tomatoes that resist cracking and can tough it out in high heat and humidity. Give it a try. Grow at least one plant. You'll be hooked in no time.

Alex Hitt and his wife, Betsy, have been farming tomatoes in North Carolina for more than thirty years. "Back in the day," said Alex, "no one knew about different varieties. We grew the hybrid Celebrity and the local tomato was German Johnson. Things changed after Cherokee Purple, my personal favorite, was introduced. We've tried over 150 varieties over the years. We're on a constant search for great flavor and better disease resistance."

## About This Book

Sometime back, I told a friend that I was writing a book on southern tomatoes. He pondered that a moment and then quipped, "So just a bunch of tomato recipes with a whole lot of mayonnaise?"

I laughed and explained that this book features recipes highlighting tomatoes with a southern heritage and sensibility. While a recipe cannot talk, it does have a history, so it can, in a way, speak. Certain dishes fit into a culture, can tell a story; they can remind you of a moment in time, a person, a place. Tomatoes can remind you of the South.

A tomato absolutely becomes southern when it's sliced thick, salted well, given a righteous slathering of Duke's, slapped between two slices of floppy white bread, and eaten over the kitchen sink. A tomato also becomes southern when it's gently stewed with onions, sweetened with the tiniest bit of sugar, and served in a bowl with buttered bread cubes or baked under buttered slices of bread. When it's simmered with okra and bacon. When it's fried in butter in a black skillet with "green" corn. When it's sliced and layered in a piecrust, spread with mayonnaise, sprinkled with cheese, and baked. When it's made into a conserve. When it's simmered with rice.

A tomato becomes southern when it's green and sliced and crumbed in cornmeal and fried in bacon drippings. Even if the first tomato was fried in Italy. Even if the first southern recipes for fried tomatoes called for ripe, red tomatoes. The first known recipe for fried green tomatoes in a southern cookbook appeared in 1875 in *Housekeeping in the Blue Grass: A New and Practical Cook Book*, edited by the Ladies of the Presbyterian Church of Paris, Kentucky. This book was subsequently republished in 1904 as *The Blue Grass Cook Book*, compiled by Minnie C. Fox.

According to food historian and cookbook author Damon Lee Fowler, "Cookbooks then reflected the past; in the old days, if a recipe was in print, it had already been in use for a generation." Here is the fried green tomato recipe as it appeared in 1875:

Slice the tomatoes and lay in salt water a half hour, drain and roll in corn-meal, and fry in hot lard; salt and pepper to taste. —*Miss Short.*

Not so different from today. Get out your skillets!

# A Note

In many recipes, I've made suggestions for the type of tomatoes to use. Please regard these as suggestions only. Let the market and the season dictate which tomatoes you choose—whatever's ripe and whatever looks and tastes best. Also, some recipes call for canned tomatoes as a first choice or an alternate. Plus, I've indicated which recipes add spark to even out-of-season tomatoes.

Thankfully—just like people—not all tomatoes are the same size. What seems medium in one variety (or on one day) might be considered closer to large in another. They're just not uniform, and that's why we love them.

In many recipes, I've provided the number of tomatoes, the weight (please use scales; they're your kitchen friends), and the cup measurement, just so there's no confusion. In some cases, like for salads, a few tomatoes more or less makes no difference. But for baked items, where something could bubble over or not bake properly, or in preserving, please use the amount indicated for best results.

# Starters and Soups

Opening with the best ever Bloody Mary, a zippy tomato aspic, and a perfect cream of tomato soup, here is where we start our tomato journey. These recipes only begin to highlight the versatility of this vegetable (which is really a fruit). You don't even have to grow your own or wait for tomato season because all the soups but the Green Tomato and Bacon Soup may be made with top-quality canned tomatoes.

# Bloody Mary

*The quintessential tomato quencher is the Bloody Mary. This recipe makes enough for four because it's a sociable drink. Make it fancy by rubbing a lime wedge around the rim of each glass and "frosting" it in a plate of coarse salt or Cajun seasoning. And you may omit the vodka, of course. If you add the splash of pickled okra brine, garnish the drinks with pickled okra. It's more fun than a celery stick! This is even better made with my Fresh-Brewed Tomato Juice (page 122).*

MAKES 4 DRINKS

---

4 cups chilled tomato juice

¼ cup lime juice, plus lime wedges for garnish

2 tablespoons peeled, finely grated horseradish

1 teaspoon Worcestershire sauce

½ teaspoon kosher salt, or to taste

½ teaspoon Cajun seasoning

5–6 grinds of the pepper mill

2–4 dashes Tabasco sauce, or to taste

Splash of pickled okra brine (optional)

Lots of ice cubes

6–8 ounces vodka

---

Pour the tomato juice into a pitcher. Mix in the lime juice, horseradish, Worcestershire sauce, salt, Cajun seasoning, pepper, Tabasco sauce, and okra brine, if you like.

Fill 4 tall glasses with ice. Pour the Bloody Mary mixture and 1½–2 ounces vodka into each glass. Stir, add lime wedges, and serve.

## CHOOSING TOMATOES

When buying tomatoes, handle them with care. You'd reject a bruised one, so don't spoil them for the next customer.

At a farmers' market I often visit, a farmer parked a six-pack of toilet paper among his baskets of tomatoes. The message was clear: Squeeze this, not that.

Look for tomatoes with smooth skins and no bruising, seepage, or cracks. Sniff for a fragrance, a pleasant one. Pick those that are heavy for their size. It's better to buy tomatoes a little on the firm side. Soft ones will no doubt turn to mush on the way home, especially when chucked into a plastic sack. If you can, purchase tomatoes in the basket they're displayed in or ask that they be put in a paper bag. Or better yet, bring your own basket.

At the supermarket, if they're not in a plastic container (not environmentally friendly, I know, but it keeps them from bruising), pack them in a doubled plastic bag, tie it closed, and watch where the cashier puts them.

If needed, ripen tomatoes at home in a single layer on a baking sheet or platter. They can be left outside in a shady spot but not in the sun. Never, ever refrigerate tomatoes, which will blunt their flavor. The only exception is very ripe cherry tomatoes, which you should refrigerate and use up as soon as possible.

# Heirloom Tomato Stacks with Clemson Blue Cheese Dressing and Bacon Crumbles

*This is a stellar first course to serve when the tomatoes are at their peak—heavy, ripe, and juicy. Clemson Blue is an artisanal cheese that's made in small amounts at Clemson University, in the Piedmont area of South Carolina. Any other mild blue cheese may be substituted. Use locally produced, wood-smoked bacon, if you can get it.*

MAKES 4 FIRST-COURSE SERVINGS

---

½ cup sour cream

¼ cup mayonnaise

1 tablespoon fruity extra-virgin olive oil

2 teaspoons white wine vinegar

½ teaspoon freshly ground black pepper

¼ teaspoon kosher salt

¼ teaspoon Worcestershire sauce

⅓–½ cup crumbled Clemson Blue cheese

1 tablespoon thinly sliced chives or scallion greens

1 bunch arugula or watercress, rinsed and spun dry

5–6 large, ripe heirloom tomatoes, such as Cherokee Purple, Delicious, Striped German, or Brandywine (2½ pounds), cored and cut crosswise into ½-inch-thick slices

4 thick bacon slices, cooked until crisp and crumbled

---

Mix the sour cream, mayonnaise, olive oil, vinegar, pepper, salt, and Worcestershire sauce in a small bowl with a whisk or fork. Stir in the blue cheese and chives or scallions.

Divide the arugula or watercress between 4 plates. Stack the tomato slices on the greens, leaning a little, and sprinkle lightly with a little more salt and pepper. Spoon the dressing on top and crumble the bacon over the tomatoes. Serve.

# Creamy Corn Custard
# with Fresh Tomato Salsa

*The salsa that's served alongside the corn custard started out as a nice but uninspired chopped salsa. When I saw it was going to be too watery because the tomatoes were so juicy and ripe, I got out my skillet and reduced it to a delicious, flavorful sauce. It now holds its own yet blends beautifully with the custard.*

*Prepare the salsa after the custard goes into the oven or a bit earlier. The custard dish is placed in a waterbath, which provides steam and a cushion from the heat of the oven so the custard becomes silky and creamy. Serve as a first course or for a light supper dish.*

MAKES 6 FIRST-COURSE SERVINGS AND 1½ CUPS SALSA

**FOR THE CUSTARD**

2½ cups corn kernels, including the "milk" from the cobs, divided

2 teaspoons cornstarch

1½ cups heavy cream, divided

6 large eggs

1 tablespoon granulated sugar

2 teaspoons kosher salt

2–3 teaspoons green Tabasco sauce

½ cup thinly sliced scallions

**FOR THE SALSA**

3 large, ripe heirloom tomatoes, such as Brandywine or
   Cherokee Purple (1½ pounds), grated (about 2 cups)

½ cup chopped red onion

2 tablespoons lime juice

1 jalapeño pepper, minced, with some or all of the seeds

1 teaspoon ground cumin

¾ teaspoon kosher salt

1 tablespoon canola or olive oil

½ cup chopped cilantro

Preheat the oven to 350°. Butter a 9-inch square baking dish.

Put ½ cup of the corn in a food processor and pulse 2 or 3 times to chop coarsely. Mix the cornstarch and 3 tablespoons of the cream in a cup, stirring well to dissolve the cornstarch.

Whisk the eggs, sugar, salt, and Tabasco sauce in a large bowl until well blended. Whisk in the cornstarch mixture and remaining cream. Stir in the processed corn, whole kernels, and scallions. Scrape into the prepared baking dish. Place the baking dish into a larger metal baking pan or roasting pan. Pull out the middle oven rack, place the baking pan on the rack, and pour about ½ inch of hot water into the larger pan.

Bake the custard until lightly puffed, firm at the edges, and just a little jiggly in the center, 30–40 minutes. Carefully remove it from the waterbath and place it on a wire rack. Let stand for 30 minutes before serving.

Meanwhile, to make the salsa, put the grated tomatoes in a medium bowl and stir in the red onion, lime juice, jalapeño, cumin, and salt.

Warm the oil in a heavy, medium skillet over high heat until very hot but not smoking. Carefully pour in the tomato mixture. Cook, stirring often, until the sauce has thickened and is a deeper red, 13–15 minutes. Cool. Stir in the cilantro. Serve the custard with the salsa.

### GRATING TOMATOES

This easy method reduces a tomato to pulp in no time.

Place a four-sided box grater in a pie plate to collect the juices. Starting with the bottom end, rub the tomato on the coarse holes of the grater until nothing is left but skin and a little bit of core, watching your fingers carefully.

# Tomato Aspic

*I confess I did not grow up eating tomato aspic, deemed "the ultimate party dish" by southern food writer James Villas.* In the hilarious volume Being Dead Is No Excuse: The Official Southern Ladies Guide to Hosting the Perfect Funeral *by Gayden Metcalfe and Charlotte Hays, we learn that in the Mississippi Delta, tomato aspic must be served at the reception following a funeral. It's considered essential for "dying tastefully." Therefore, no self-respecting book on southern tomatoes would be complete without a recipe for tomato aspic, served, of course, with homemade mayonnaise. Some like it chunky, like me and Mrs. S. R. Dull, author of the standard,* Southern Cooking, *and Lee Bailey, whose recipe was the inspiration for this one. Some like it smooth, like my Savannah-born friend, Margaret Shakespeare.*

*Another friend, Carroll Leggett, who was born in Bertie County, North Carolina, said his mother never made it. "It was considered sort of fancy and bridge club food where I came from. Never saw it at a church event. We had no electricity when I was born; we had oil lamps and an icebox. No one wanted to be running around in the heat with tomato aspic."*

MAKES 8–12 FIRST-COURSE OR SIDE-DISH SERVINGS

---

3 envelopes unflavored gelatin

⅔ cup cold water

4 cups tomato juice

1 tablespoon plus 1 teaspoon granulated sugar

1 teaspoon kosher salt

½ teaspoon Worcestershire sauce

¼ cup lime or lemon juice

1–2 tablespoons prepared white horseradish

1 tablespoon cider vinegar

½ teaspoon Tabasco sauce, or more to taste

½ cup finely chopped tender inner celery stalks,
    plus ¼ cup chopped tender celery leaves

½ cup finely chopped peeled hothouse cucumber,
  plus sliced cucumber for garnish
½ cup finely chopped red or green bell pepper
¼ cup finely chopped Vidalia onion
Soft lettuce leaves and parsley sprigs, for garnish
  (optional garnishes include ripe or pimiento-stuffed
  olives and cooked shrimp)
Homemade Mayonnaise, for serving (page 54)

Sprinkle the gelatin over the cold water in a small bowl. Stir briefly. Let stand for 5 minutes to bloom.

Stir together the tomato juice, sugar, salt, and Worcestershire sauce in a medium saucepan over medium heat and bring just to a boil. Remove from the heat and add the gelatin mixture, stirring until completely dissolved. Pour into a large metal bowl and stir in the lime or lemon juice, horseradish to taste, vinegar, and Tabasco sauce to taste. Refrigerate, uncovered, until it starts to thicken slightly, 1 hour to 1 hour and 30 minutes.

Generously oil an 8- to 10-cup gelatin ring mold or Bundt pan. Gently fold the celery and celery leaves, chopped cucumber, bell pepper, and onion into the thickened tomato juice. Pour into the prepared mold. Cover with foil and refrigerate overnight until firm.

To unmold, dip the mold briefly in hot water, then wipe off the outside with a towel. Place a silver platter over the mold and turn both over together, giving a sharp shake to loosen the aspic. You might need to let it sit a moment until it falls out. If it doesn't, repeat the brief dipping, as above. Surround the aspic with lettuce leaves and garnish with parsley sprigs, cucumber slices, and other garnishes, if desired. Serve with Homemade Mayonnaise.

NOTE ❋ To transport this dish on a hot day, leave the aspic in the mold and place it and the mayonnaise and garnishes in a cooler with ice. Pack your silver platter and unmold the aspic at the reception.

# Very Classy Cream of Tomato Soup

*This is what cream of tomato soup is supposed to taste like but (almost) never does. Ladle it into your best china bowls for a starter at a snazzy dinner, or serve it in everyday earthenware for a casual lunch. Grilled cheese with tomato is perfect on the side. Out of season, use canned tomatoes. Straining the soup creates a rich, velvety texture, so don't skip this step.*

MAKES 6 SERVINGS

---

6 large, ripe, meaty tomatoes, such as Amish Paste,
    Celebrity, or German Johnson (3 pounds), peeled, cored,
    and seeded, cut into rough pieces (about 5½ cups), or 2
    28-ounce cans whole tomatoes in juice, drained
3 tablespoons unsalted butter
1 large onion, chopped (about 1 cup)
2 tablespoons plus 1½ teaspoons all-purpose flour
2 cups whole milk
½ cup half-and-half
2½ teaspoons kosher salt (1½ teaspoons if using canned
    tomatoes)
1 teaspoon granulated sugar
¼ teaspoon freshly ground black pepper

---

Purée the fresh or canned tomatoes in a food processor, in batches if necessary. You'll get about 4 cups foamy, pink purée (closer to 3½ cups for canned).

Melt the butter in a Dutch oven over medium heat. Add the onion and cook, stirring often, until tender, about 5 minutes. Add the flour and cook, stirring, for 2 minutes; it will turn golden in spots. Gradually whisk in the milk and half-and-half, about ½ cup at a time. Cook, whisking often, until it thickens and just comes to a boil. Reduce the heat and simmer, stirring often and scraping the sides, for 3 more minutes.

Whisk in the puréed tomatoes, salt, sugar, and pepper. Bring to a boil over medium heat, stirring often so it doesn't scorch. Remove from the heat.

Strain the soup through a fine-mesh strainer suspended over a large saucepan, pressing down on the solids. Reheat over medium heat, stirring often. Taste for seasoning. Serve hot.

## PEELING AND SEEDING TOMATOES

Some cookbooks instruct you to score an X on the bottom of a tomato before blanching it, which means plunging it into boiling water. Please don't. It's a waste of time. Also, if the skin is scored, water will seep in and could quickly produce a mealy, mushy, waterlogged tomato. For an uncooked or lightly cooked dish, the flavor and texture will be compromised.

*Peeling*: Bring a large or medium saucepan of water to a boil. Rinse the tomatoes. Add 3 or 4 to the boiling water. Blanch, turning once, for 20–30 seconds. They're ready when the skin on the side feels loose or starts to wrinkle. Transfer to a baking pan with a slotted spoon. Riper and smaller tomatoes will be ready sooner. If the skin still isn't loose, dunk the tomato back in the water for another 10 seconds.

When the tomatoes are cool enough to handle, using a small, sharp knife, cut out the core, the fibrous, dimpled bit where the tomato was attached to the stem. Careful—the tomatoes can be slippery. You can also use a tomato corer. Then, with your fingers and the knife, peel off the skin.

*Seeding*: Cut the peeled tomato crosswise in half. Working over a bowl, gently squeeze the tomato without crushing it, then shake it a little so the seeds fall out. You can also dislodge seeds with your fingers or a teaspoon. You'll never remove all of the seeds, but don't worry—the seeds have lots of flavor.

# Curried Tomato Soup

*Good hot or cold, this soup may be prepared with fresh or canned tomatoes. Serve it in small portions topped with a cooling spoonful of Greek yogurt. You don't have to seed the fresh tomatoes here, unless they're awfully seedy. If they are, remove only some seeds or you won't have enough tomato.*

*To prepare the lemongrass, cut off and discard about 2 inches of the bulb end. Pull off the tough outer leaves and slice only the tender end part, stopping when the stalk feels fibrous. Chop finely. You'll need about 3 stalks of lemongrass.*

MAKES 6–8 SERVINGS

½ teaspoon cumin seeds
1 teaspoon ground coriander
¾ teaspoon kosher salt
½ teaspoon turmeric
¼ teaspoon freshly ground black pepper
⅛ teaspoon cinnamon
⅛ teaspoon cayenne pepper
3 tablespoons olive oil
1 large onion, finely chopped (about 1 cup)
1½ tablespoons finely chopped lemongrass
1 tablespoon peeled, finely grated ginger
1 large garlic clove, minced
5–6 large, ripe, meaty tomatoes, such as Amish Paste, Celebrity, or German Johnson (2½ pounds), peeled, cored, and cut into ½-inch chunks (about 5 cups), or 2 28-ounce cans diced tomatoes in juice, drained (about 4 cups)
2 cups reduced-sodium chicken broth
3 tablespoons tomato paste
Plain Greek yogurt, for serving

Toast the cumin seeds in a small skillet over medium heat, stirring often, until fragrant and a little darker in color, about 3 minutes. Tip into a bowl and cool. Grind with a mortar and pestle or crush with the bottom of a small, heavy pan. Mix in the coriander, salt, turmeric, black pepper, cinnamon, and cayenne pepper.

Heat the olive oil in a Dutch oven over medium heat. Add the onion and cook, stirring often, until tender, about 4 minutes. Stir in the lemongrass, ginger, garlic, and spice mixture. Cook, stirring, until fragrant, about 1 minute.

Stir in the tomatoes, chicken broth, and tomato paste; increase the heat and bring to a boil. Reduce the heat to low, cover, and simmer for 20 minutes. With an immersion blender or in batches in a food processor, process the soup to a slightly chunky texture. Reheat or chill, and taste for seasoning. Ladle into bowls and top each with a spoonful of yogurt. Serve.

# Tomato Dumpling Soup

*I'm not sure of the heritage of this soup, but it may be Pennsylvania Dutch. My connection to it is strictly romantic. I first tasted it while being courted by my husband-to-be at a now-closed restaurant, the Willow Inn. Situated in an old farmhouse in southwestern Pennsylvania, it was owned by two men who, sadly, are no longer with us.*

*Pat Varner was host, headwaiter, and creator of the folksy paintings that adorned the walls. The chef, Ralph Wilson, was always a little gruff, and there was no asking for a recipe. There was no menu either, just an elaborate multicourse dinner, whatever Ralph felt like cooking that day. The dishes were always rich and a little over-the-top, like this soup, which was served in a white china tureen, scented with cinnamon, and crowned with light, eggy dumplings.*

*After some searching, I found the recipe in an e-newsletter published by the Cactus Cablers, a sewing club in Tucson, Arizona, specializing in the "smocking arts." One of the members must have come from southwestern Pennsylvania. And somehow, she got the recipe from the chef, who apparently got it from an old issue of* Gourmet.

MAKES 6–8 SERVINGS

**FOR THE SOUP**

2 28-ounce cans whole tomatoes in juice, drained
(1½ cups juice reserved)
6 tablespoons unsalted butter
½ large Vidalia onion, coarsely chopped (about 1½ cups)
1 medium-large green bell pepper, coarsely chopped (1 cup)
2½ cups reduced-sodium chicken broth
2 tablespoons granulated sugar
2 tablespoons tomato paste
1½ teaspoons cinnamon
1¼ teaspoons kosher salt

½ teaspoon freshly ground black pepper
2 tablespoons thinly sliced chives or chopped flat-leaf parsley,
   for garnish

FOR THE DUMPLINGS
¾ cup all-purpose flour
¾ teaspoon baking powder
¼ teaspoon fine table salt
2 large eggs
1 tablespoon plus 1 teaspoon canola oil

To make the soup, purée the tomatoes with the reserved juice,
in batches if necessary, in a food processor.

Melt the butter in a Dutch oven over medium heat. Stir in
the onion and bell pepper, cover, and cook, stirring occasionally,
until tender, 8–10 minutes. Add the puréed tomatoes, chicken
broth, sugar, tomato paste, cinnamon, salt, and pepper. Whisk
until blended. Increase the heat and bring to a boil. Reduce the
heat to low and simmer, uncovered, stirring often, for 10 minutes, until the flavors are blended.

To make the dumplings, stir together the flour, baking powder, and salt in a large bowl. Add the eggs and oil and beat
vigorously with a spoon until well blended. The batter will be
sticky. Drop heaping ½ teaspoons of the batter on top of the
simmering soup. (They won't be round; instead they'll be a little
lumpy-looking, but that's fine.)

Cover the soup and simmer over low heat, without stirring,
until the dumplings are firm and cooked through, about 15 minutes. Ladle into bowls, sprinkle each with some chives or parsley, and serve.

NOTE ✳ Any leftover soup will thicken in the refrigerator. Add a little
broth or water when reheating.

## A CORING CONUNDRUM

Recipe terms don't necessarily mean the same thing to every cook. I discovered this when a good friend kindly agreed to retest a couple of recipes. One recipe said to core and slice green tomatoes. To my surprise, my friend removed all of the "guts" from the tomatoes before slicing, leaving only curls of skin with a little inner flesh.

In an informal poll, I asked others what they thought a recipe meant when it said to core a tomato. They replied that they thought it was akin to coring an apple with an apple corer, meaning much more of the tomato would be scooped out and discarded than intended.

For the record, coring a tomato means to remove only the fibrous bit where it once was attached to the stem. You can use a paring knife. You can use a neat tool called a tomato corer, which has little serrated teeth and a short handle. You can slice the tomato in half lengthwise and cut a V with a knife in each half to remove the core. You can cut the to-mato in wedges and slice off the bit of core at the tip of each wedge. When the core is tiny, you can ignore it. But please, unless the recipe says to seed tomatoes or hollow them out, as for filled tomatoes, leave the insides inside.

# Green Tomato and Bacon Soup

*Here's a great use for those tart green tomatoes and a perfect meal for a chilly evening. Add cornbread or biscuits and some fruit or a salad. Green tomatoes are sometimes available at the grocery store. Just ask the produce manager; the store might have them "ripening" in the back. This soup freezes well.*

MAKES 4–6 SERVINGS

---

3 thick bacon slices, cut into rough ¼-inch pieces

½ large Vidalia onion, chopped (about 1½ cups)

1 medium green bell pepper, coarsely chopped (about ¾ cup)

1 large carrot, coarsely chopped (about ¾ cup)

2 large garlic cloves, minced

½ teaspoon dried thyme

½ teaspoon kosher salt

¼ teaspoon freshly ground black pepper

5 medium green tomatoes (1½ pounds), cored and coarsely chopped (about 4½ cups)

2 cups reduced-sodium chicken broth

1 cup water

---

Cook the bacon in a Dutch oven over medium heat, stirring often, until all the fat is rendered, 6–8 minutes. Spoon off all but 2 tablespoons of the drippings, leaving the bacon in the pan.

Add the onion, bell pepper, carrot, and garlic to the drippings and cook, stirring often, until the vegetables are nearly crisp-tender, about 5 minutes. Stir in the thyme, salt, and pepper. Add the green tomatoes and mix well.

Add the chicken broth and water; increase the heat and bring to a boil. Reduce the heat to low, cover, and simmer until the tomatoes are very tender and the flavors are blended, 25–30 minutes. If you like, crush the tomatoes with a potato masher to make the soup thicker and more cohesive. Taste for seasoning. Serve hot.

# Tomato Salads

I'm the first to admit that you don't need a recipe to make a simple and wonderful tomato salad, just a sharp slicing knife, some coarse salt, and a plate. But if you want to take things a step further, make the salad a bit sassier, read on. In this chapter, you'll find a terrific version of a favorite cuke-onion-tomato combo, a couple of restaurant-elegant tomato salads to wow friends and family, and a new southern tradition, Tomato and Watermelon Salad with Feta and Oregano.

# Wilted Cucumbers with Tomatoes

*This salad is found on lunch and supper tables throughout the cucumber and tomato season. You can marinate the tomatoes with the cucumbers, if you wish, but I prefer folding them in right before serving so they don't get mushy. And if it's not tomato season, don't despair; this salad is still tasty made with thin-skinned, sweet, round supermarket tomatoes and hothouse cucumbers.*

MAKES 4–6 SIDE-DISH SERVINGS

---

3 medium, slender, thin-skinned cucumbers or
    1 long hothouse cucumber (about 1¼ pounds)
1 teaspoon kosher salt
2 tablespoons fruity extra-virgin olive oil
2–3 tablespoons white wine vinegar or cider vinegar
1 tablespoon granulated sugar
¼ teaspoon freshly ground black pepper
½ medium Vidalia or other sweet white onion,
    thinly sliced (1 cup)
4–6 small-to-medium, firm-but-ripe, sweet tomatoes,
    such as Stupice or West Virginia (1 pound), cored and
    cut into thin wedges (about 3 cups)

---

Cut cucumbers into ⅛-inch-thick slices (you'll get about 3½ cups). Put in a colander set in a bowl and mix with the salt. Place plastic wrap directly over the cucumbers, then top with a plate that fits just inside the colander. Place a large can (like a can of tomatoes!) on top to weigh the cucumbers down. Refrigerate for 1 hour. Remove the can and plate. Press down gently on the cucumbers to release any more liquid, then discard the liquid.

Mix the olive oil, 2 tablespoons of the vinegar, the sugar, and the pepper in a serving bowl, stirring to dissolve the sugar. Stir in the cucumbers and onion. Cover and refrigerate for at least 30 minutes or overnight (if overnight, drain off some of the accumulated liquid the next day).

Gently mix in the tomatoes and taste, adding the remaining 1 tablespoon vinegar and seasoning with additional salt and pepper if you wish. Serve.

## VOLUNTEER TOMATOES

One year, our garden was full of tomato volunteers. These tiny plants sprouted everywhere from seeds, born, no doubt, in the compost, where we chuck the food and garden waste. I weeded out most of them because often volunteers don't grow true. Generally, they become some sort of cherry tomato. But one patch looked so robust and healthy I let it grow. It became a crazy vining maze bearing the sweetest, most delightful fruits that hung on forever. They were perfect in Wilted Cucumbers with Tomatoes (page 34). I wish I'd saved some seeds.

# Tomatoes, Mozzarella, and Roasted Peppers with Red Onions and Sherry Vinegar

*Use the best, most fragrant heirloom tomatoes in this elegant salad, my personal riff on a Caprese. Fresh, milky mozzarella and fruity, grassy olive oil are necessities as well. In a pinch, pick up some roasted peppers from the supermarket's deli section. For fun, add a ripe-when-green tomato, such as Aunt Ruby's German Green or Cherokee Green, into the mix. A combination of opal and Genovese basil adds an aromatic touch. In other words, use this recipe as a guide.*

MAKES 4 FIRST-COURSE SERVINGS

---

2 medium red bell peppers

3 tablespoons fruity extra-virgin olive oil

1 tablespoon plus 1 teaspoon sherry vinegar

1 tablespoon lemon juice

1 teaspoon honey

1 teaspoon coarse sea salt or kosher salt

1/8 teaspoon freshly ground black pepper

1/2 small red onion, thinly sliced (about 1/2 cup)

2–3 very large, ripe heirloom tomatoes, such as Brandywine, Cherokee Purple, or a bicolor, such as Old German or Mr. Stripey (about 1 1/2 pounds)

8 ounces fresh mozzarella, sliced

1/4 cup finely slivered basil, plus basil sprigs for garnish

---

Roast the bell peppers directly over the flames of a gas burner or under a broiler, turning often, until the skins are charred and blistered, 12–15 minutes. Transfer to a bowl. Cover with a dish towel so they steam and cool for about 20 minutes. Peel off the skins with your fingers and a paring knife. Cut the peppers in half and remove the cores and seeds. Cut the peppers into ½-inch-thick strips.

Mix the olive oil, vinegar, lemon juice, honey, salt, and pepper in a medium bowl with a fork. Add the pepper strips and red onion; toss to mix. Let marinate for 15 minutes.

Meanwhile, blanch and peel the tomatoes. Halve and core them and cut them crosswise into ½-inch-thick slices. Arrange on a medium platter with sides to catch all the juices. Season lightly with additional salt and pepper and layer the mozzarella on top. Spoon the marinated onions and peppers over, adding the dressing from the bowl. Sprinkle with the slivered basil and garnish with basil sprigs. Let stand for 10–15 minutes to let the flavors blend before serving.

# Currant Tomato and Butterbean Salad with Lemon Vinaigrette and Crisp Garlic Toasts

*I'm proud to include this recipe, developed by my friend Sheri Castle. A terrific food writer, Sheri penned* The New Southern Garden Cookbook: Enjoying the Best from Homegrown Gardens, Farmers' Markets, Roadside Stands, and CSA Farm Boxes. *She told me about a tiny tomato that grows wild in her North Carolina garden called the Cumberland Cascade Currant.*

*"These volunteer each summer," she said, "rangy and roaming. They spread all over the place like a low shrub if not corralled. The fruit is profuse, growing in tight clusters like grapes, and the tomatoes are impossibly small, their flavor the perfect melding of fruity and acidic." Sheri said she has to almost stand on her head to pick them, but it's one of those garden labors of love. They are only suitable for use in a salad and are lovely combined with creamy, freshly shelled butterbeans. If you can't find these babies, choose another cherry tomato.*

MAKES 6 LUNCHEON OR LIGHT-SUPPER SERVINGS

**FOR THE VINAIGRETTE**
Finely grated zest of 1 large lemon
¼ cup lemon juice
2 large garlic cloves, minced
1 large shallot, minced
½ teaspoon granulated sugar
¼ teaspoon kosher salt
¾ cup fruity extra-virgin olive oil
¼ teaspoon Dijon mustard
Freshly ground black pepper, to taste

3 cups freshly shelled butterbeans

1 small onion, quartered, root left on

2 small bay leaves

6 flat-leaf parsley sprigs, plus 2 tablespoons chopped leaves

4 short thyme sprigs, preferably lemon thyme

1 whole allspice berry

1 whole clove

1 teaspoon kosher salt

1 tablespoon fruity extra-virgin olive oil

3 cups whole currant tomatoes or small halved cherry
    tomatoes

2 tablespoons finely chopped mint

1/2 teaspoon freshly ground black pepper

FOR THE TOASTS

6 large (1/2-inch thick) slices crusty country-style bread,
    halved diagonally

Extra-virgin olive oil, for drizzling

1 large garlic clove, peeled and halved

---

To make the vinaigrette, put the lemon zest and juice, garlic, shallot, sugar, and salt in a small jar with a tight-fitting lid. Let sit for 10 minutes, then shake gently to blend. Add the olive oil and mustard; shake vigorously. Season with pepper and more salt, if needed. Shake before using.

To make the salad, place the butterbeans in a medium saucepan; cover with 2 inches cold water. Add the onion, bay leaves, parsley and thyme sprigs, allspice, and clove. Bring just to a boil, skim off any foam, reduce the heat, and simmer gently, uncovered, until the beans are almost tender, 15–20 minutes, depending on their size.

Remove from the heat; stir in the salt. Let sit for 15 minutes until the beans are fully tender (but not mushy or falling apart). Drain well. Transfer to a large bowl; toss with the olive oil and cool to room temperature. Pick out and discard the onion, bay leaves, herb sprigs, and whole spices.

Meanwhile, mix the tomatoes and vinaigrette in a medium bowl. Let sit as the beans cool, stirring occasionally. Add to the beans with the chopped parsley, mint, and pepper. Stir gently and taste for seasoning.

To make the toasts, preheat the broiler. Drizzle both sides of the bread generously with olive oil. Arrange on a baking sheet. Broil, turning once, until crisp and golden brown on the outside but still slightly chewy in the center, about 3 minutes. Immediately rub the garlic over one side of each slice. Place 2 pieces on each of 6 salad plates. Spoon the salad over the top and serve.

# Heirloom Tomato Salad

*I patterned this after a salad I devoured at Crook's Corner restaurant in Chapel Hill, North Carolina, during high tomato season. Every bite was perfection. The combination of tomatoes was stunning, each contributing a different taste—sweet, tangy, tart, and sassy. Choose tomatoes that aren't sloppy-ripe; they should have a touch of crispness.*

MAKES 4 FIRST-COURSE SERVINGS

---

3–4 large, ripe, juicy heirloom tomatoes, such as Brandywine, Cherokee Purple, Oxheart, or German Johnson (2 pounds), peeled if you like

4–6 very small, firm yellow pear or ripe-when-green tomatoes, such as Green Zebra (8 ounces)

1 cup halved cherry tomatoes, such as Sungold or Sweet 100's

½ small Vidalia or sweet red onion, thinly sliced (about ½ cup)

2 tablespoons fruity extra-virgin olive oil

2 teaspoons balsamic vinegar

1 teaspoon lemon juice

1 teaspoon coarse sea salt or kosher salt

2 tablespoons finely slivered basil, plus basil sprigs for garnish

---

Quarter the large tomatoes, cut off the cores, and slice crosswise ½-inch thick. Arrange on a medium platter with sides to catch all the juices. Quarter the small yellow or green tomatoes and arrange casually over the tomato slices. Scatter the cherry tomatoes and onion on top.

Mix the olive oil, vinegar, lemon juice, and salt in a cup with a fork. Spoon the dressing over the salad and sprinkle with the slivered basil. Garnish with basil sprigs. Let stand for a few minutes to let the flavors blend before serving.

# Peach and Tomato Salad
# with Toasted Pecans

*"I hear a symphony," sang Diana Ross and the Supremes. You'll hear one too — or taste one — when you dig into this southern symphony in a bowl. The idea was born during a cool, cloudy summer when tomatoes would not seem to ripen. Now I make it every year because the peaches brighten the tomatoes, even if the tomatoes are full of flavor. No need to peel the peaches unless the skins are very thick and fuzzy. Try it with nectarines too. And it might be wonderful with the yellow tomatoes that resemble peaches and have soft, fuzzy skins. They're called Yellow Peach.*

MAKES 4 FIRST-COURSE OR SIDE-DISH SERVINGS

½ cup pecan halves

1 tablespoon fruity extra-virgin olive oil

1 tablespoon honey

2 teaspoons lemon juice

1 teaspoon champagne or white wine vinegar

¼ teaspoon kosher salt

⅛ teaspoon freshly ground black pepper

2 tablespoons finely chopped shallot or red onion

3 medium, firm-but-ripe peaches (1 pound), peeled if you like
and cut into thin wedges (about 3 cups)

2–3 medium, firm-but-ripe purple or red heirloom tomatoes,
such as Black Krim, Eva Purple Ball, or Stupice (1 pound),
cored and cut into thin wedges (about 3 cups)

2 tablespoons finely slivered mint leaves

1 tablespoon finely slivered opal or Thai basil, or regular basil

Preheat the oven to 400°.

Put the pecans in a small baking pan and bake, stirring several times, until toasted, 10–12 minutes. Tip into a bowl and let cool, then break them up with your fingers.

Mix the olive oil, honey, lemon juice, vinegar, salt, and pepper with a fork in a shallow serving bowl. Stir in the shallot or red onion. Let stand for a few minutes to blend the flavors.

Add the peaches, tomatoes, mint, and basil; toss gently. Let stand for 5 minutes. Taste, adding a little more lemon juice, if you wish. Sprinkle with the toasted pecans and serve.

## GROWING TOMATOES

This is a book-size subject, but if you're just starting out, here are some general tips.

*Start with a plant*: Instead of starting from seed, beginners should buy plants at a good nursery, ask plenty of questions, and read the tags, making sure to choose the right tomato for your climate. Tomatoes need full sun. Check at home that you have enough sun and stufficient space.

*Growing tomatoes in pots*: Many types of tomatoes grow well in pots, and more dwarf varieties are being developed. According to Barbara Melera from D. Landreth Seed Company, most tomatoes do very well in pots because they don't get soil-borne diseases. However, many tomato plants grow quite large and all grow for a long time, so be sure the pot is big enough and in the right location before you begin.

*Planting the tomato*: When you get the plant home, if it's going in the ground or a pot, plant it as soon as possible. Choose a warm, overcast day so it doesn't get sunscald, basically a sunburn. Early evening is good, as is a light rain. Wind is not good since strong wind could break a delicate plant.

For each plant, dig a deep hole and work about 2 tablespoons organic fertilizer or some compost or well-aged manure into the soil. (If planting in a pot, prepare loose soil the same way.) Remove the plant from its container and place it in the hole up to the bottom leaf. Add a small stake for support and label it. Firm the soil around it, and water the soil but not the plant itself.

*It needs support*: Not emotionally, but physically, with a cage or bamboo or other poles—something to grow on. If you don't have cages, tie the vines as they grow to the poles or stakes; strips of old stockings work great. The vines can be delicate, yet the tomatoes get very heavy.

*Can it sprawl on the ground?*: Yes, in many cases, but I don't. In a damp year, tomatoes touching the wet ground will rot or be invaded by insects. Splashing soil from rain or heavy watering can spread disease. I like to keep the plant well off the ground.

*While the plant grows*: Don't use chemicals. Don't fertilize all the time. I might fertilize once more after planting, and my garden has heavy clay soil. Don't let it dry out, but don't overwater it. You're supposed to water about 1 inch per week, but I have never figured out how to judge that. Water in the morning, before the heat, and avoid watering the leaves. Uneven watering causes blossom-end rot, which is as awful as it sounds. Drip irrigation is great.

*The big ugly tomato worm*: There are few tomato pests, outside of deer and groundhogs. Aphids can be a problem. Control them with insecticidal soap, used sparingly. The other pest is the tomato hornworm, a huge tomato-vine green caterpillar that will eat nearly a plant a day. Often, they're found after you see the damage. Look for their large (for a caterpillar) blocky droppings. Cut off the piece of plant they're on and squish them, unless they're dotted with white bits and look as if they're drying up, which means parasitic wasps are attacking them. These beneficial insects will do the killing for you, so you can just leave them be.

Lots of things can happen to tomatoes. But most of the time, they just provide plenty of succulent fruit, better than anything you can buy.

# Tomato and Watermelon Salad
# with Feta and Oregano

*Once when we were driving through rural North Carolina, my husband and I spotted grocery carts filled with fat watermelons parked in front of a funky gas station. The weather was scorching, and a wedge of one of those melons would surely have refreshed. This salad is for the dog days. It's a marriage of the sweetness and acidity of the fruit (remember, tomatoes are a fruit too) with the sharp bite of onion and the salty tang of the feta and olives. Use a pink tomato so the color mirrors that of the watermelon.*

MAKES 4 FIRST-COURSE OR SIDE-DISH SERVINGS

---

2 large, ripe heirloom tomatoes, preferably pink, such as German Johnson, Barnes Mountain Pink, or June Pink (1 pound), quartered, cores cut off, and cut crosswise into ¼-inch-thick slices (about 3 cups)

¼ of a small seedless watermelon (cut lengthwise in a long wedge) (about 1¼ pounds), rind removed and cut crosswise into ¼-inch-thick slices (about 3 cups)

2 tablespoons fruity extra-virgin olive oil

2 teaspoons red wine vinegar

½ teaspoon coarse sea salt or kosher salt

¼ teaspoon freshly ground black pepper

4 ounces coarsely crumbled excellent-quality feta cheese

8 whole calamata olives, sliced off the pits

3 tablespoons thinly sliced red onion

½ teaspoon dried Turkish or Mexican oregano

---

Combine the tomatoes and watermelon in a shallow serving bowl. Drizzle with the olive oil and vinegar and sprinkle with the salt and pepper. Toss gently.

Strew the feta, olives, and red onion over the salad. Crumble the oregano on top. Taste for seasoning and serve.

# Sandwiches, Spreads, and Filled Tomatoes

Tomato sandwiches and BLTs start off this chapter, which includes other luncheon favorites such as tomatoes filled with ham salad and tomatoes stuffed with a luscious crabmeat rémoulade. Plus there are recipes for a rich (and easy) Homemade Mayonnaise and a delicious Olive Oil Sandwich Loaf for cooks who want to have the best and start from scratch. For snacks or appetizers to serve with toasts or crackers or as sandwich spreads, there are two tasty recipes: Baby Plum Tomato and Olive Tapenade and Matbucha, a spicy Moroccan tomato dip.

# Stand-over-the-Sink
# Tomato Sandwiches

*On a visit to Chapel Hill, North Carolina, we dined with friends at Crook's Corner. As soon as we were seated, the chef sent over a platter of tomato sandwiches. We all dove in, leaving not even a crumb behind.*

*Done casually on Harris Teeter white bread cut into quarters with the crusts left on, the sandwiches were paved with an inch of Hellmann's, Chef Bill Smith's mayo of choice and, as he told us, what his grandmother always used. They were the most perfect way to begin a wonderful summer meal. You can make these with my Homemade Mayonnaise (page 54) or your mayo of choice, and you can put them on my Olive Oil Sandwich Loaf (page 52). Or not.*

MAKES 2 SANDWICHES

---

2–3 large, ripe, juicy heirloom tomatoes, such as Cherokee Purple, Brandywine, German Johnson, Mr. Stripey, or your favorite slicer (about 1½ pounds), peeled if you like

Coarse sea salt or kosher salt and freshly ground black pepper, to taste

About ¼ cup Homemade Mayonnaise (page 54) or store-bought mayonnaise

4 slices white bread, of your choice

---

Core the tomatoes and cut into thick or medium-thick slices, discarding (okay, eating) the ends. Sprinkle the tomatoes with salt and pepper to taste. Spread the mayonnaise on the bread, as thick as you dare. Place the tomato slices on 2 of the bread slices; place the other 2 bread slices on top. Cut the sandwiches into halves or quarters. Pick up one half or quarter, lean over the sink, and devour.

## VICKSBURG TOMATO SANDWICHES

In Vicksburg, Mississippi, at tea parties, Junior League or Junior Auxiliary events, ladies luncheons, wedding showers, and club meetings, a very special tomato sandwich is served. It's not the messy, lean-over-the-sink type. Instead, it's very neat, dainty finger food. And in this part of the historic South, it's a tradition. It goes without saying that these are arranged on doilies on silver platters.

The tomatoes are first peeled (it's bad form not to) and sliced thin, about ¼ of an inch. These tomatoes should be evenly round and the right diameter so the slices fit just inside a round cut from a slice of white bread. The tomato slices are first drained on a double layer of paper towels, so their juices *do not* soak through the sandwiches, and then seasoned with salt and pepper.

Day-old white bread is cut into rounds with a biscuit cutter and spread with homemade mayonnaise. A round is topped with a tomato slice, a little more salt and pepper, ½ teaspoon grated onion with a little juice, and another round of bread. Often sandwiches are made earlier in the day and stored on waxed paper–lined baking sheets, with sheets of waxed paper between the layers. Before serving, they're sprinkled with paprika.

Marcie Cohen Ferris, author of *Matzoh Ball Gumbo: Culinary Tales of the Jewish South*, mentioned to me a "hot" variation on light bread with spicy mayonnaise. She claimed you could eat a zillion of them. Thanks to Marcie and to *Vintage Vicksburg*, a cookbook compiled by the Junior Auxiliary of Vicksburg.

# Classic BLT

*Whoever came up with the combination of crisp, just-fried bacon; juicy, dead-ripe tomatoes; soft lettuce; and mayonnaise on toasted bread was a genius. No one is ever unhappy with a good BLT. Not even vegetarians, who make do with just the lettuce and tomatoes.*

*Everyone seems to have his or her own twist, but mine is plenty classic. I prefer tender garden lettuce with its herby, green flavor, which softens and blends into the sandwich instead of staying wet and fighting it (read iceberg). I also adore sweet onions on my BLTs, and I prefer them open-face; the second slice of bread simply gets in the way and blunts the flavor. It's also filling. I'd really rather have another sandwich. Also, you can't easily "adjust" a closed-face sandwich. Like adding a little more salt or positioning the bacon to get some in every bite. Speaking of bacon, use the best you can get.*

MAKES 2 SANDWICHES

4–6 thick bacon slices

2–4 large slices crusty country-style bread, (multi-grain or cracked-wheat is good)

About ¼ cup Homemade Mayonnaise (page 54) or store-bought mayonnaise

2 large, ripe heirloom tomatoes, such as Brandywine, Cherokee Purple, German Johnson, or your favorite slicer (about 1 pound)

About 1 cup soft, mild lettuce leaves

Few slices Vidalia onion or other crisp, sweet white or red onion (optional)

Coarse sea salt or kosher salt and freshly ground black pepper, to taste

Fry the bacon in a cast-iron skillet over medium-low heat, turning once, until crisp and golden, 8–10 minutes. Drain on a double layer of paper towels.

Toast the bread slices and spread with mayonnaise. Core the tomatoes and cut into ½-inch-thick slices, discarding or eating the ends. On two slices of toast, layer lettuce, tomato slices, and a little onion, if you like. Season to taste with salt and pepper and arrange the bacon on top. If desired, place another slice of toast on top, pressing down lightly, and cut the sandwich in half. If it's open-face, leave it whole. Serve right away.

NOTE ✻ If you're feeding a crowd, multiply everything as needed and put all the fixings on platters. Serve on the porch or picnic table and provide tons of napkins and a pitcher of sweet tea.

# Olive Oil Sandwich Loaf

*Many favor soft, store-bought white bread to enclose fat slices of tomato slathered with mayo, but I like my tomato sandwiches on a bread with more presence, with a firmer crumb and a finer flavor. Try the rosemary variation, especially for tomato sandwiches. Rising times will vary depending on the heat of your kitchen. The olive oil glaze gives the loaves a matte finish, and the egg glaze adds a high shine. The choice is yours.*

MAKES 2 LOAVES

---

¼ cup warm water (105°–110°)

1 envelope or a scant tablespoon active dry yeast

½ teaspoon granulated sugar

2¼ cups lukewarm water

½ cup fruity extra-virgin olive oil

1 tablespoon plus 1½ teaspoons kosher salt

7–8 cups white bread flour or all-purpose flour

3 tablespoons chopped rosemary leaves (optional)

Additional olive oil or 1 egg yolk beaten with 1 tablespoon
   whole milk, for glaze

---

Put the warm water in the large bowl of a stand mixer fitted with a paddle (or a large bowl). Stir in the yeast and sugar. Let stand until the yeast is frothy, about 10 minutes. (If it isn't, throw it out and try again with cooler water and/or fresher yeast.)

Mix in the lukewarm water, olive oil, and salt. Add 2 cups of the flour and beat slowly at first, then on medium speed, until well mixed and creamy (if mixing by hand, use a whisk). Scrape the bowl and paddle.

On low speed (or with a wooden spoon), add 4 more cups of flour, about ½ cup at a time, beating just until mixed—it may look lumpy. Mix in the rosemary, if using.

Switch over to a dough hook as the dough becomes harder to mix (or transfer the dough to a floured work surface). Knead the dough on low speed, adding flour as necessary, about a tablespoon at a time, until smooth and elastic, about 8 minutes. If machine-kneaded, turn it out onto a work surface and finish kneading by hand until silky, 1–2 more minutes.

Coat a large bowl with olive oil. Place the dough in the bowl and turn it over to oil the surface. Cover the bowl with plastic wrap and let the dough rise at room temperature until doubled in bulk, 45 minutes to 1 hour and 15 minutes.

Grease two 8 ½ × 4 ½-inch loaf pans with shortening.

Gently punch down the dough. Turn it out onto a lightly floured surface and cut it in half. Pat each half into a rectangle about 9 inches long. Roll up tightly from the long side, tucking the ends under. Place each loaf seam-side down in a prepared pan. Cover the pans with cotton or linen dish towels. Let rise at room temperature until the dough just swells over the tops of the pans, 45 minutes to 1 hour and 30 minutes.

Meanwhile, preheat the oven to 375°.

Brush the tops of the loaves with olive oil or the egg glaze. Bake until well browned and hollow-sounding when tapped on the bottom, 40–45 minutes. Turn out of the pans, place directly on the oven rack, and bake until the bottom crust is browned, about 5 more minutes. Transfer the loaves to a wire rack to cool completely.

# Homemade Mayonnaise

*I like to use a combination of olive oil and a neutral-flavored oil, such as canola, in this recipe because I find olive oil alone too over-powering. You may, of course, make it with only canola oil. May-onnaise can be flavored with chopped herbs such as dill, parsley, or chives, or enhanced with minced garlic and more lemon juice or lemon zest. Or try curry powder and lime zest. For spicy may-onnaise, add Cajun seasoning and/or Sriracha and maybe a bit of orange zest. Refrigerate mayonnaise promptly after making it, and use it up soon. If it starts to get too thick during processing, do what the pros do: add a touch of warm water.*

MAKES ABOUT 1 ¼ CUPS

---

Yolk from 1 large egg

2 tablespoons lemon juice

2 teaspoons water

1 teaspoon Dijon mustard

½ teaspoon kosher salt

¾ cup canola oil or other neutral oil, such as safflower
   or grapeseed

¼ cup fruity extra-virgin olive oil

---

Put the egg yolk, 1 tablespoon of the lemon juice, the water, the mustard, and the salt in a food processor. Process just to blend (you may have to mix it a little with a spatula). With the machine running, pour the oils through the feed tube in a slow, steady stream, adding another tablespoon lemon juice (and maybe some warm water) about halfway through if it starts to get too thick.

When all the oil has been added, taste, adding more lemon juice or salt, if you like. Cover and refrigerate.

# Filled Tomatoes
# with Crabmeat Rémoulade

*For a striking presentation, spoon this luxurious salad into black or orange tomatoes. Fresh tarragon can be very mild, so I've given a range for the amount. Rémoulade is a classic New Orleans sauce that's wonderful with the sweet crabmeat.*

MAKES 4 LUNCHEON SERVINGS

⅓ cup Homemade Mayonnaise (page 54) or store-bought mayonnaise

2–3 tablespoons chopped tarragon

2 tablespoons chopped flat-leaf parsley

1 tablespoon chopped drained capers

1 tablespoon lemon juice

1½ teaspoons Creole or grainy Dijon mustard

¾ teaspoon sweet paprika

1 small garlic clove, finely minced or grated

Pinch of cayenne pepper, or to taste

8 ounces crabmeat, picked over for shells

1 hard-boiled egg, chopped

2 scallions, thinly sliced

4 medium, firm tomatoes (about 6 ounces each)

Stir together the mayonnaise, 2 tablespoons of the tarragon, and the parsley, capers, lemon juice, mustard, paprika, garlic, and cayenne pepper to taste in a medium bowl. Add the crabmeat, egg, and scallions and mix gently. Taste for seasoning, adding a little salt or more tarragon or cayenne pepper, if you wish.

Slice the tops off the tomatoes. With a melon baller, remove the insides of the tomatoes to make a shell. Gently press your fingers inside the tomato shells to squeeze out any remaining seeds or juice. Place the tomatoes on a serving platter with sides to hold them upright or in a baking dish. Spoon about ½ cup crab salad into each and serve.

# Filled Tomatoes with Ham and Bread-and-Butter Pickle Salad

*This is a wonderful way to use up ham that's left over from a picnic or summer party. The tomato serves as an edible vessel for the salad, but if you like, skip the fuss and serve it more simply with sliced ripe tomatoes. Add a basket of hot biscuits or fresh-baked cornbread to round out the meal. Use excellent bread-and-butter pickles, preferably from a home-canner's pantry. Make the ham salad early in the day so the flavors have time to blend. Serve any extra on the side.*

MAKES 4 LUNCHEON SERVINGS

---

2 cups finely chopped ham

¾ cup bread-and-butter pickles, drained (1 tablespoon juice reserved) and chopped

⅓ cup Homemade Mayonnaise (page 54) or store-bought mayonnaise

2 tablespoons finely chopped Vidalia onion or thinly sliced scallions

2 tablespoons chopped flat-leaf parsley or dill (or 1 tablespoon of each)

1 teaspoon Dijon mustard

Freshly ground black pepper, to taste

4 medium, firm tomatoes (about 6 ounces each)

---

Mix together the ham, pickles and pickle juice, mayonnaise, onion or scallions, parsley and/or dill, and mustard in a medium bowl. Season with plenty of pepper, to taste. Cover and refrigerate for at least 2 hours or until ready to serve.

Slice the tops off the tomatoes. With a melon baller, remove the insides of the tomatoes to make a shell. Gently press your fingers inside the tomato shells to squeeze out any remaining seeds or juice. Place the tomatoes on a serving platter with sides to hold them upright or in a baking dish. Spoon about ½ cup ham salad into each and serve.

# Baby Plum Tomato and Olive Tapenade

*This is based on a recipe from Emeril Lagasse. He used large plum tomatoes, but baby plum tomatoes, especially Black Plums, become intensely rich and sweet when roasted. Black Plum tomatoes are now a staple in my garden, almost too prolific. But they hang around long after others are done producing, so they end up in a lot of dishes. You can also make this with the large multicolored cherry tomatoes found at supermarkets or farmers' markets.*

*This is delicious spread on thin slices of toasted Italian bread or on focaccia. Add ham, goat cheese, or mozzarella for a more substantial appetizer or hearty sandwich.*

MAKES 6 APPETIZER SERVINGS

1 pound baby plum tomatoes, such as Black Plum or Juliet, halved (about 3 cups)
2 large garlic cloves, minced
1 tablespoon fruity extra-virgin olive oil
2 teaspoons finely chopped rosemary leaves
½ teaspoon kosher salt
¼ teaspoon freshly ground black pepper
⅓ cup pitted, chopped calamata olives
¼ cup chopped flat-leaf parsley
1 tablespoon drained, chopped capers

Preheat the oven to 425°.

Mound the tomatoes on a rimmed baking sheet. Add the garlic, olive oil, rosemary, salt, and pepper and toss to coat. Arrange the tomatoes cut-side down. Bake until soft and very juicy, 15–20 minutes. Let cool on the baking sheet.

With a slotted spoon, transfer one-third of the tomatoes to a cutting board. Chop them coarsely and scrape into a medium serving bowl. (Yes, this gets a little sloppy.) Repeat with the remaining tomatoes and scrape any remaining juices from the baking sheet into the bowl. Stir in the olives, parsley, and capers. Cover and refrigerate for at least 1 hour to firm up the tapenade. Taste for seasoning. Serve chilled.

# Matbucha

*This saucy, spicy cooked dip of tomatoes, roasted peppers, and sweet paprika originated in Morocco and is very popular today in Israel. Most often, matbucha is served as a mezze, or appetizer selection, which includes olives and other spreads, such as hummus, with pita bread or crackers. I especially like it as a spicy accent spooned alongside fried eggs or atop a feta cheese omelet. Matbucha is a nice thing to make when you've got lots of tomatoes and they're tasty but don't have perfect texture; it also freezes well. Out of season, use canned tomatoes.*

MAKES 8–10 APPETIZER SERVINGS

1 large red bell pepper

1 medium-large green bell pepper

1/3 cup olive oil

1 large red onion, halved and thinly sliced (1 1/2 cups)

4–5 large garlic cloves, minced

2 teaspoons sweet paprika

1 1/2–2 teaspoons Aleppo pepper, or to taste

3/4 teaspoon granulated sugar

3/4 teaspoon kosher salt

1/2 teaspoon freshly ground black pepper

1/2 teaspoon ground cumin

5–6 large, ripe, meaty tomatoes, such as Amish Paste, Oxheart, or Rutgers (2 1/2 pounds), peeled, cored, and cut into 1-inch chunks (about 5 cups) or 2 28-ounce cans tomatoes in juice, drained (1 1/2 cups juice reserved), cut into 1-inch chunks

Roast the bell peppers directly over the flames of a gas burner or under a broiler, turning often, until the skins are charred and blistered, 12–15 minutes. Transfer to a bowl. Cover with a dish towel so they steam and cool for about 20 minutes. Peel off the skins with your fingers and a paring knife. Cut the peppers in half and remove the cores and seeds. Cut into rough ½-inch pieces.

Heat the olive oil in a large, heavy, deep skillet or Dutch oven over medium heat. Add the red onion and garlic and cook, stirring often, until tender, 5–6 minutes. Add the paprika, Aleppo pepper, sugar, salt, black pepper, and cumin and cook, stirring, for 1 minute. Stir in the roasted peppers.

Add the fresh tomatoes (or canned tomatoes and reserved juice) and bring to a boil. Reduce the heat to medium-low and simmer, uncovered, stirring often, until the vegetables are very tender and the mixture is saucy and thick but not too dry, about 40 minutes. Transfer to a serving dish, cover, and refrigerate; it thickens as it cools. Taste again before serving.

# Main Dishes, Pies, Casseroles, and Cobblers

Tomatoes star in all manner of dishes in this chapter, from savory tomato pies, to garlic grits, a double-corn cobbler, chopped and seasoned tomatoes baked under crunchy bread, and a squash casserole. I think of these as my go-to recipes, always reliable, always crowd-pleasing. I make them often, with pride, for potlucks, brunches, or Sunday supper.

# Open-Face Tomato Pie

*My husband adores anything baked in or under a crust. This pie was definitely a hit, with its double layer of juicy tomatoes, crisp, cheesy crumbs, and creamy herbed mayonnaise. Avoid the urge to use more tomatoes than the recipe calls for or the pie won't heat through properly. Cut it with a good serrated bread knife or a pie cutter. The first piece is never perfect.*

MAKES 4 MAIN-DISH SERVINGS

---

Pastry for a 9-inch single-crust pie (can be store-bought)

4–5 medium, firm-but-ripe tomatoes, such as Stupice or Arkansas Traveler (1½ pounds)

¾ teaspoon kosher salt, divided

1¼ cups shredded sharp white cheddar cheese, divided

½ cup plain panko crumbs

¼ cup thinly sliced red onion

¾ cup mayonnaise

⅓ cup chopped basil

2 tablespoons thinly sliced chives

¼ teaspoon freshly ground black pepper

---

Preheat the oven to 375°.

Fit the pastry into a 9-inch pie plate and form a high, fluted edge. Prick all over with a fork. Put a sheet of foil inside the pastry and fill the foil with dried beans or rice. Bake until the pastry is set and white at the edges, 10–12 minutes. Remove the foil with the beans or rice, return the pastry to the oven, and bake until it's brown in spots, 8–10 more minutes. If it starts to slip down, press it back in place with a spoon. Cool on a wire rack.

Halve and core the tomatoes and cut them crosswise into ¼-inch-thick half-moon slices, discarding the ends. (You should have a heaping 3 cups.) Place the tomato slices on a double layer of paper towels and sprinkle with ½ teaspoon of the salt. Let stand for about 5 minutes.

Toss ½ cup of the cheddar with the panko crumbs in a small bowl. Sprinkle half of this evenly over the bottom of the cooled crust. Arrange half of the tomatoes in an overlapping circle on top of the crumbs, filling the center with more tomato slices. Sprinkle with half of the red onion and ¼ cup of the cheddar. Arrange the remaining tomatoes in the same manner on top; sprinkle with the remaining red onion.

Mix the mayonnaise, basil, chives, remaining ½ cup cheddar, pepper, and remaining ¼ teaspoon salt in another small bowl. Spread over the tomatoes with a rubber spatula, covering them completely, using your fingers to help since the mixture is thick. Sprinkle with the remaining crumb-cheese mixture.

Bake the pie until the top is browned and the filling has started to bubble at the edges, 45–50 minutes. Transfer to a wire rack and let stand for at least 30 minutes for easiest cutting. Serve warm or at room temperature, cut into wedges.

# Green Tomato and Pork Tenderloin Biscuit Pie

*Seasoned like a delicious breakfast sausage, this pie has larger, more toothsome chunks of tender pork. For a streamlined production, get the crust organized first: Mix the dry ingredients, crumble in the butter, and set the bowl in the fridge. Next, prepare the filling and keep it warm. Then finish making the biscuit dough, roll it out, and place it over the hot filling.*

MAKES 6 MAIN-DISH SERVINGS

### FOR THE FILLING

1 pound trimmed pork tenderloin, cut into ½-inch chunks

2 tablespoons olive oil, divided

1¾ teaspoons kosher salt

1 teaspoon freshly ground black pepper

1 teaspoon dried sage

¼–½ teaspoon crushed red pepper flakes

⅛ teaspoon allspice

6 ounces cremini or baby portabello mushrooms, halved and thinly sliced (2½ cups)

1 large onion, chopped (about 1 cup)

3 tablespoons all-purpose flour

5 medium green tomatoes (1½ pounds), cored and cut into ½-inch pieces (about 4½ cups)

1 cup reduced-sodium chicken broth

### FOR THE CRUST

1½ cups all-purpose flour, plus extra flour for rolling

2 teaspoons baking powder

½ teaspoon fine table salt

6 tablespoons cold unsalted butter, cut into small pieces

About ½ cup cold milk

1 tablespoon melted unsalted butter

Preheat the oven to 425°.

Put the pork in a medium bowl. Add 1 tablespoon of the olive oil and the salt, black pepper, sage, crushed red pepper, and allspice and toss to coat the pork well.

Heat the remaining 1 tablespoon olive oil in an 11-inch (2-inch-deep) cast-iron skillet over medium-high heat until hot but not smoking. Add the pork, leaving it undisturbed for 1 minute. Then cook, stirring often, until lightly browned but still pink in the center, 3–4 minutes. Add the mushrooms and onion and cook, stirring often, until the mushrooms are tender, about 4 minutes. Stir in the flour.

Add the green tomatoes and toss to mix. Add the chicken broth, stir well, and bring to a boil. Reduce the heat to low. Cover and simmer, stirring occasionally, until the tomatoes are mostly tender and the juices are lightly thickened, 10–12 minutes. Cover and set aside.

To make the crust, stir together the flour, baking powder, and salt in a large bowl. Add the cut-up butter and crumble it in with your fingers or cut it in with a pastry blender until the mixture forms coarse crumbs. Stir in enough of the milk to make a medium-soft dough. Fold the dough over itself in the bowl 3–4 times, until cohesive.

Flour a work surface and rolling pin. Roll and pat the dough to a 10-inch round, about ¼-inch thick. Brush off any excess flour.

Place the crust over the hot filling. Cut 2 or 3 slits in it to allow steam to escape. Brush with the melted butter. Bake until the crust is browned and crisp and the filling is bubbly at the edges, 20–25 minutes. Let it stand for a few minutes before serving.

NOTE ❉ Since the pie may bubble up during baking, position one oven rack in the middle of the oven and another rack beneath. Set a rimmed baking sheet on the lower rack, under the skillet, to catch any drips.

# Double Corn and Tomato Cobbler

*Use fresh corn, leftover cooked corn cut off the cob, or thawed frozen kernels. A deep, ovenproof, stainless-steel-lined skillet is ideal for making this vegetarian main dish. Avoid cast-iron because it will react with the acid in the tomatoes.*

MAKES 4 MAIN-DISH SERVINGS

### FOR THE FILLING

2 tablespoons olive oil

2 large or 3 medium sweet Italian frying peppers, halved lengthwise, seeded, and sliced crosswise 1/4-inch thick (about 1 1/2 cups)

1 large onion, coarsely chopped (about 1 cup)

2 garlic cloves, minced

1/4–1/2 teaspoon crushed red pepper flakes

3/4 teaspoon kosher salt, divided

4 large, ripe, meaty tomatoes, such as Amish Paste, Oxheart, or Celebrity (2 pounds), cored and cut into 1 1/2-inch chunks (about 6 cups)

1 cup halved Sungold or other orange or red cherry tomatoes

1/2 teaspoon freshly ground black pepper

### FOR THE COBBLER TOPPING

3/4 cup stone-ground yellow cornmeal

3/4 cup all-purpose flour

1 1/2 teaspoons baking powder

1/2 teaspoon baking soda

1 teaspoon granulated sugar

3/4 teaspoon kosher salt

1/4 teaspoon freshly ground black pepper

3 tablespoons cold unsalted butter, cut into small pieces

1 cup corn kernels

3/4 cup buttermilk, plus more, if needed

Preheat the oven to 425°.

To make the filling, heat the olive oil in a heavy, ovenproof, 10- to 11-inch (2½-inch deep) skillet over medium heat. Add the frying peppers, onion, garlic, and crushed red pepper and ½ teaspoon of the salt. Cook, stirring often, adding a tablespoon of water if the vegetables start to stick, until tender, 6–8 minutes. Add the big tomatoes, cherry tomatoes, remaining ¼ teaspoon salt, and black pepper. Cook, stirring frequently, until the tomatoes start to soften (but they should not break down) and the skins begin to curl, 4–5 minutes. Remove from the heat. Cover to keep warm.

To make the cobbler topping, stir the cornmeal, flour, baking powder, baking soda, sugar, salt, and pepper in a large bowl. Rub in the butter with your fingertips or a pastry blender until the mixture is crumbly. Mix in the corn. Add the buttermilk and stir just until a soft dough forms. Add additional buttermilk, 1 tablespoon at a time, if it seems dry.

Dollop heaping tablespoons of the batter on the hot filling. Bake until the cobbler topping is firm and lightly browned and a toothpick inserted in the center comes out clean, 20–25 minutes. Serve hot.

# Baked Garlic-Cheese Grits
## with Tomato-Crunch Topping

*A wonderful brunch dish, this would also be a welcome contribution to a covered-dish supper. Small- to medium-sized very sweet tomatoes work best. Supermarket tomatoes, such as Campari, work well also because the baking brings out their flavor.*

MAKES 6 MAIN-DISH SERVINGS

**FOR THE GRITS**

3 cups water

1½ teaspoons kosher salt

¾ cup stone-ground grits

4 tablespoons unsalted butter

2–3 large garlic cloves, minced

1 cup thinly sliced scallions or ½ medium Vidalia onion, chopped (about 1 cup)

2 cups shredded sharp white cheddar cheese

2 large eggs

¾ teaspoon freshly ground black pepper

**FOR THE TOPPING**

8–12 small, sweet, round tomatoes or about 8 small Roma tomatoes (1¼ pounds), cored and cut crosswise into thin slices (about 2½ cups)

½ cup plain panko crumbs

½ cup freshly grated Parmesan cheese

2 tablespoons unsalted butter, cut into small pieces

Preheat the oven to 350°. Butter an 8 × 12-inch glass baking dish.

To make the grits, bring the water to a boil in a large heavy saucepan. Add the salt, then whisk in the grits in a steady stream. Bring to a boil. Reduce the heat to low, cover, and simmer, stirring occasionally, until the grits have thickened and are creamy, 15–20 minutes. Remove from the heat.

Melt the butter in a medium skillet over medium heat. Add the garlic and cook, stirring, until fragrant, 1–2 minutes. Add the scallions or onion and cook, stirring often, for 2–4 minutes, until tender (onion takes longer). Scrape into the grits. Add the cheddar, eggs, and pepper and beat with a wooden spoon until the mixture is well blended and the cheese has melted. Scrape into the prepared baking dish.

To make the topping, arrange the tomatoes in overlapping rows on the grits. Mix the panko crumbs, Parmesan, and butter in a small bowl, crumbling it with your fingers until blended and mixed into coarse crumbs. Sprinkle over the tomatoes.

Bake, uncovered, until the topping is browned and crisp and the grits are bubbling at the edges, 30–35 minutes. Let stand for 10 minutes before serving.

NOTE ❈ You can prepare the grits, smooth them into the dish, cover, and refrigerate for up to 2 days prior to serving. Slice the tomatoes and make the crunch topping just before the casserole goes in the oven. It may take a few minutes longer to heat through.

# Goat Cheese Spoonbread
# with Cherry Tomato Sauté

*I love this cheesy twist on spoonbread, which is really a light, moist, cornmeal soufflé. The cherry tomato sauté is the perfect juicy accompaniment—it complements the flavors but doesn't get in the way. It is also a delightful way to cook cherry tomatoes and enhances the flavor of supermarket cherry tomatoes. While spoonbread is usually served "on the side," with butter, or as a vehicle to sop up rich gravy, this one can take pride of table as the main event at brunch or a light lunch. It's even good reheated.*

MAKES 6 SIDE-DISH OR 4 MAIN-DISH SERVINGS

### FOR THE SPOONBREAD
3 tablespoons unsalted butter, at room temperature, divided
¾ cup freshly grated Parmesan cheese, divided
2 cups whole milk
1 cup stone-ground white or yellow cornmeal
1 teaspoon baking powder
1 teaspoon kosher salt, plus a pinch for the egg whites
4 large eggs, separated
8 ounces soft, fresh goat cheese, cut into pieces

### FOR THE CHERRY TOMATOES
2 tablespoons unsalted butter
1 garlic clove, minced
⅓ cup chopped flat-leaf parsley
4 cups halved cherry or grape tomatoes, any color
¼ teaspoon kosher salt
⅛ teaspoon freshly ground black pepper

To make the spoonbread, preheat the oven to 375°. Coat a 2-quart, 8-inch square glass baking dish with 1 tablespoon of the butter and dust with ¼ cup of the Parmesan.

Heat the milk in a large, heavy saucepan over medium heat until it just starts to bubble. Whisk in the cornmeal in a slow, steady stream. Bring to a boil and cook, stirring frequently, for 1 minute. Remove from the heat.

With a wooden spoon, beat in the remaining 2 tablespoons butter, baking powder, and salt. Beat in the egg yolks, then the goat cheese, a few pieces at a time, and then the remaining ½ cup Parmesan, stirring vigorously until well blended.

Beat the egg whites and a pinch of salt in a medium bowl with an electric mixer at high speed until stiff, glossy peaks form when the beaters are lifted.

Stir a big spoonful of the whites into the cornmeal mixture to lighten it. Fold in the remaining whites with a large rubber spatula. Scrape into the prepared dish.

Bake until the spoonbread is puffed and firm to the touch and the top is browned, 30–35 minutes.

To make the cherry tomatoes, about 10 minutes before the spoonbread is ready, melt the butter in a large, heavy skillet over medium heat. Stir in the garlic, then the parsley. Cook, stirring, until fragrant, about 1 minute.

Add the cherry tomatoes, salt, and pepper and toss to mix well. Increase the heat and cook, stirring often, until the tomatoes collapse, 4–5 minutes. Taste for seasoning. Cover and keep warm. Cut the spoonbread into pieces and spoon some cherry tomatoes alongside.

# Edna Lewis's Baked Tomatoes
# with Crusty Bread

*This was inspired by Edna Lewis's recipe in* Gourmet *magazine's southern food issue.* When I lived in New York, I often saw Miss Lewis at the Union Square Greenmarket, looking serene and regal, with long, dangling earrings, her beautiful white hair pulled into a bun.

A church supper favorite, this is a recipe you'll turn to often. The version I was more familiar with had a topping of scattered bread cubes. This is better. The entire surface is paved with buttery bread slices, which become crusty and delicious as they bake. Miss Lewis called for good-quality bakery bread, so you could use my Olive Oil Sandwich Loaf (page 52), but if you use softer bread, slice it a little thinner. I like it best with crusty Italian bread, but some types can get crisp quickly, so pay attention as this bakes.

MAKES 6 SIDE-DISH SERVINGS

---

6 tablespoons unsalted butter, divided

½ medium red onion, chopped (about 1 cup)

½ teaspoon kosher salt

2 tablespoons granulated sugar

2 garlic cloves, minced

1 teaspoon dried thyme, crumbled

½ teaspoon freshly ground black pepper

¼ teaspoon allspice

2 28-ounce cans diced tomatoes in juice, drained
(1½ cups juice reserved)

6–7 slices (½-inch thick) crusty Italian country-style bread
(about 5½ inches wide)

---

Preheat the oven to 425°. Butter an 8 × 12-inch glass baking dish.

Melt 2 tablespoons of the butter in a large, heavy, deep skillet over medium heat. Add the red onion and salt and cook, stirring often, until lightly golden, 6–8 minutes. Add the sugar, garlic, thyme, pepper, and allspice and cook, stirring, for 1 minute. Add the tomatoes and reserved tomato juice and bring to a boil. Reduce the heat and simmer briskly, uncovered, stirring occasionally, until thickened and reduced, but not dry, about 10 minutes. Scrape into the prepared dish.

Meanwhile, melt the remaining 4 tablespoons butter in a microwave or a small saucepan. Generously brush the butter on both sides of each slice of bread and cut each slice in half diagonally. Place the bread on top of the tomatoes, overlapping the slices to cover the tomatoes completely. Bake until the bread is lightly golden and crisp and the tomatoes are bubbly, 20–30 minutes. Serve hot.

# Tomato-Squash Casserole

*Bored with packaged bread-crumb toppings and thinking that panko crumbs didn't quite work here, I asked my buddy Fred Thompson, crack southern cookbook author, for a suggestion. He had a great one: whole wheat Ritz crackers ground in a food processor or crushed in a plastic bag with a rolling pin. They add a delicious nuttiness to this casserole, which can be served as a side dish or a vegetarian entrée.*

MAKES 6–8 SIDE-DISH OR 4 MAIN-DISH SERVINGS

¾ cup ground whole wheat Ritz crackers, divided

1 teaspoon kosher salt

½ teaspoon freshly ground black pepper

4–5 mixed small zucchini and yellow summer squashes
(1½ pounds), cut into ¼-inch-thick rounds (about 5 cups)

½ large Vidalia onion, coarsely chopped (about 1½ cups)

6–8 medium, firm-but-ripe tomatoes, such as Rutgers,
Arkansas Traveler, or Black Prince (2 pounds), cored and
cut crosswise into ¼-inch-thick slices (about 5 cups)

2 tablespoons coarsely chopped thyme leaves

2 cups shredded sharp white cheddar cheese

1 cup shredded Swiss cheese

3 tablespoons unsalted butter, cut up

Preheat the oven to 375°. Generously butter a 13 × 9-inch glass baking dish. Dust the bottom of the dish with ¼ cup of the cracker crumbs. Mix the salt and pepper in a cup.

Layer half of the squashes in the baking dish. Sprinkle with half of the onion and arrange half of the tomato slices on top. Sprinkle with half of the salt and pepper mixture and half of the thyme.

Mix the cheddar and Swiss. Sprinkle half of the cheese mixture over the vegetables and repeat the layers of squash, onion, and tomatoes, sprinkling them with the remaining salt and pepper and thyme. Top with the remaining cheese. Sprinkle the remaining ½ cup cracker crumbs on top and dot with the butter.

Bake, uncovered, until the casserole is browned and bubbly and the vegetables are tender, 45–50 minutes. Let stand for 10 minutes before serving.

# Tomatoes on the Side

Fried Green Tomatoes headline this chapter, but read on to find more great "receipts" for favorite southern classics, such as Fried Corn with Cherry Tomatoes, stewed tomatoes, tomatoes and okra, and Savannah Red Rice. Serve them on the side or as starters or make them the focus of the meal, with cornbread or biscuits and a salad.

# Fried Green Tomatoes

*Coat these just before frying and eat them right away or they'll become soggy, especially if the tomatoes are "pink" or partially ripened (which are especially yummy).* In Damon Lee Fowler's *wonderfully informative book,* Classical Southern Cooking, *and in subsequent conversations, he explained that often, people fried tomatoes in all stages of ripeness, seasoning them with sugar and salt and adding the essential flavor ingredient to the frying medium—bacon drippings. That's what I've used here, along with some canola oil, because, as Damon writes, "Yes, you must use some bacon drippings." Setting the fried tomatoes on a rack in the oven while you fry the rest is another of Damon's inventive techniques to keep them crisp and delicious.*

MAKES 4 FIRST-COURSE OR SIDE-DISH SERVINGS

1 teaspoon kosher salt
$\frac{1}{2}$ teaspoon freshly ground black pepper
$\frac{1}{2}$ teaspoon granulated sugar
5–6 medium, firm green or "pink" tomatoes (2 pounds), cored and cut crosswise into $\frac{1}{4}$-inch-thick-rounds, ends discarded
1 large egg
$\frac{1}{4}$ cup whole milk
2–3 teaspoons Sriracha hot sauce
1$\frac{1}{2}$ cups all-purpose flour
$\frac{1}{2}$ cup canola oil, or more if needed, and $\frac{1}{4}$ cup bacon drippings, for frying

Preheat the oven to 200°. Place a wire rack on a large baking sheet.

Mix the salt, pepper, and sugar in a cup and sprinkle over both sides of the tomatoes. Place the tomatoes on a double layer of paper towels. Let them stand for a few minutes.

Meanwhile, whisk the egg, milk, and Sriracha in a pie plate. Put the flour in another pie plate. Lightly blot the top surface of the tomatoes.

Dip a tomato slice into the egg mixture, letting the excess drip off. Coat both sides with flour, then transfer to a waxed paper–lined baking sheet. Repeat with the remaining tomato slices, placing waxed paper between the layers.

Heat the oil and bacon drippings in a large cast-iron skillet over medium-high heat until very hot but not smoking. Add a single layer of tomatoes. Fry, turning once, until golden brown and crisp, reducing the heat if necessary, 3–4 minutes. Remove from the skillet and drain on a double layer of paper towels. Transfer to the rack on the baking sheet. Keep warm in the oven while frying the rest. Add more oil to the skillet if needed. Serve hot.

# Cornmeal-Crumbed Fried Green Tomatoes with Buttermilk–Black Pepper Dressing

*At an Association of Food Journalist's luncheon in Charleston, South Carolina, we were served a perfect bite: a just-fried, cornmeal-dusted, crisp slice of green tomato topped with frothy pimiento cheese and a rosette of country ham. The woman next to me plucked off her ham and set it aside. I wanted to steal it.*

*This preparation is simpler than that one and doable in a home kitchen. If you have some thinly sliced country ham, do use it to adorn or accompany these fried beauties. The buttermilk dressing was inspired by one served with another dish of excellent fried green 'maters at Hominy Grill, Robert Stehling's award-winning Charleston eatery.*

*Because these have a sturdier (yet tender and crunchy) coating—unlike the flour-coated ones in the previous recipe—they have a longer life. They can be breaded up to an hour ahead and refrigerated. I've even fried them and transported them to a party, where they were reheated and devoured. They're also fabulous with Red Tomato and Jalapeño Conserve, for Nathalie (page 121).*

MAKES 4 FIRST-COURSE OR SIDE-DISH SERVINGS,
WITH ABOUT ⅔ CUP DRESSING

---

**FOR THE TOMATOES**

1 teaspoon kosher salt

½ teaspoon freshly ground black pepper

5–6 medium, firm green tomatoes (2 pounds), cored and cut crosswise into ¼-inch-thick slices, ends discarded

1½ cups stone-ground yellow cornmeal

½ cup all-purpose flour

2 large eggs

½ cup buttermilk

About ¾ cup canola oil and 6 tablespoons bacon drippings, for frying

3 tablespoons sour cream or plain Greek yogurt
3 tablespoons mayonnaise
3 tablespoons buttermilk
1 tablespoon chopped scallions
2 teaspoons dill- or sweet-pickle relish
1½ teaspoons lemon juice
½ teaspoon kosher salt
½ teaspoon freshly ground black pepper

Preheat the oven to 200°. Place a wire rack on a large baking sheet.

Mix the salt and pepper in a cup and sprinkle over both sides of the tomatoes. Place the tomatoes on a double layer of paper towels. Let them stand for a few minutes.

Meanwhile, put the cornmeal and flour in separate pie plates. Whisk the eggs and buttermilk in a shallow bowl. Lightly blot the top surface of the tomatoes.

Coat a tomato slice with flour, then dip it in the egg mixture, letting the excess drip off, then coat with the cornmeal, pressing lightly so it adheres. Transfer to a waxed paper–lined baking sheet. Repeat with the remaining tomato slices, placing waxed paper between the layers.

Heat ½ cup of the oil and 3 tablespoons of the bacon drippings in a large cast-iron skillet over medium-high heat until very hot but not smoking. Add a single layer of tomatoes. Fry, turning once, until golden brown and crisp, reducing the heat if necessary, 3–4 minutes. Remove from the skillet and drain on a double layer of paper towels. Transfer to the rack on the baking sheet. Keep warm in the oven while frying the rest. Add more oil and bacon drippings to the skillet if needed.

To make the dressing, whisk together all of the ingredients in a small bowl. Serve with the hot tomatoes.

# Crispy-Crumbed Baked Tomatoes with Pecans and Parmesan

*These are gorgeous nestled alongside a grilled or baked fish or a juicy steak or as the star of a vegetable plate. Medium-sized round tomatoes or large Romas work best, but cut Romas lengthwise in half instead of crosswise. Good-quality supermarket tomatoes work nicely because baking intensifies their flavor. Don't be tempted to use store-bought dry bread crumbs here. Making fresh ones is so simple: Tear the bread into rough 2-inch pieces and buzz it in the food processor.*

MAKES 8 SIDE-DISH SERVINGS

8 medium, firm-but-ripe tomatoes, such as Arkansas Traveler
    or Rutgers, or large Roma tomatoes (about 2½ pounds),
    halved crosswise
¾ teaspoon kosher salt, divided
¼ teaspoon freshly ground black pepper
3 tablespoons unsalted butter
½ cup chopped scallions
1 large garlic clove, minced
1½ cups fresh bread crumbs (from about 3 slices crusty
    country-style bread)
½ cup freshly grated Parmesan cheese
⅓ cup finely chopped pecans

Preheat the oven to 425°.

Arrange the tomatoes cut-side up in a baking dish just large enough to hold them. Mix ½ teaspoon of the salt and the pepper in a cup; sprinkle over the tomatoes.

Melt the butter in a medium skillet over medium heat. Brush a little butter over the cut side of each tomato, leaving some in the skillet. Bake the tomatoes, uncovered, until they are hot, begin to soften, and look juicy on top, 20–25 minutes.

Meanwhile, add the scallions and garlic to the butter remaining in the skillet. Cook over medium heat, stirring often, until the scallions are tender, about 2 minutes. Add the bread crumbs and cook, stirring, until lightly golden and crisp, 3–5 minutes. Scrape into a medium bowl. Mix in the Parmesan, pecans, and remaining ¼ teaspoon salt.

Spoon some of the crumb mixture atop each tomato half. Bake until the crumbs are browned and heated, 10–12 more minutes. Serve hot.

# Grilled Tomatoes with Garlic and Basil

*These are a little messy but delicious and fun to do when the grill is already fired up for cooking other veggies or meats. You can also try this recipe with a ripe-when-green tomato, such as an Aunt Ruby's German Green or Cherokee Green.*

MAKES 4–6 SIDE-DISH SERVINGS

---

2 tablespoons olive oil

1–2 large garlic cloves, minced

½ teaspoon coarse sea salt or kosher salt

⅛ teaspoon freshly ground black pepper

4 medium-large, firm-but-ripe, meaty tomatoes, such as
   Oxheart, Amish Paste, Rutgers, or Cherokee Purple
   (about 2 pounds), halved crosswise

1–2 teaspoons balsamic vinegar

2–3 tablespoons slivered basil (a mix of opal and Thai basil
   would be lovely)

---

Heat a barbecue grill to medium. Rub the grids with an oiled piece of paper towel.

Mix the olive oil, garlic, salt, and pepper in a large, shallow baking dish. Add the tomatoes and turn once to coat, pressing the garlic bits into the cut sides.

Place the tomatoes cut-side up on the grill. Grill until the skins start to soften and slip and the tomatoes look a little juicy on top, about 5 minutes. Carefully turn with tongs and a metal spatula and grill until the tomatoes are hot and just tender, about 2 more minutes. (If they're very ripe or messy, don't bother turning.) Transfer cut-side up to a platter. Drizzle with the balsamic vinegar, to taste. Sprinkle with the basil and serve hot.

# Fried Corn with Cherry Tomatoes

*A terrific dish, this must be made with summer's fresh, plump, sweet corn. After cooking, the corn becomes sticky, and the cherry tomatoes get even sweeter with a tart finish. Serve with grilled or fried catfish, a platter of tender pork chops, or an assortment of fresh vegetables for a memorable summer meal. A broad, flat wooden spatula is the best tool to scrape up the bits of corn that stick to the bottom of your cast-iron skillet.*

MAKES 4 SIDE-DISH SERVINGS

---

3 tablespoons unsalted butter

3 cups fresh corn kernels, including the "milk" from the cobs

½ teaspoon kosher salt, plus a pinch for the cherry tomatoes

¼ teaspoon freshly ground black pepper

2 cups halved cherry tomatoes, any color

1 tablespoon chopped basil or parsley

---

Melt the butter in a large cast-iron skillet over medium heat. Add the corn and sprinkle with the salt and pepper. Cook, stirring often, scraping the bottom of the pan, and reducing the heat when the corn begins to stick, until the corn is tender and a deeper yellow, about 10 minutes.

Add the cherry tomatoes and a pinch more salt. Reduce the heat to low and cook, stirring frequently, until the tomatoes begin to collapse and release their juices, about 6 minutes. Remove from the heat. Taste for seasoning and sprinkle with basil or parsley. Serve hot.

# Simmered Tomatoes
# with Okra and Bacon

*I like to use small, firm okra in this dish and serve it over freshly
cooked white rice. Choose a meaty tomato. Juicier ones don't hold
up as well after cooking. In Damon Lee Fowler's* Classical Southern Cooking, *he writes that African American slaves working in
white southern kitchens were the creators of this brilliant combination of vegetables. "It was their hands that wrought the magic
that made Southern cooking legendary, that put okra in the pot
with the tomatoes, that continued to slip garlic into the kettle long
after it was out of fashion in other parts of the country."*

MAKES 4–5 SIDE-DISH SERVINGS

4 thick bacon slices, cut into ¾-inch pieces

½ medium red onion, chopped (about 1 cup)

1 large garlic clove, minced

¾ teaspoon kosher salt

½ teaspoon freshly ground black pepper

¼ teaspoon dried thyme

¼ teaspoon crushed red pepper flakes

1 pound small okra, stems cut off, sliced crosswise into
   ½-inch-thick rounds

2 large, firm-but-ripe, meaty tomatoes, such as Amish Paste,
   Celebrity, or Oxheart, or 4–6 Roma tomatoes (1 pound),
   peeled, cored, and cut into ½-inch pieces (about 2 cups)

2 tablespoons thinly sliced chives

Cook the bacon in a large, heavy skillet over medium heat, stirring often, until crisp, about 8 minutes. With a slotted spoon, transfer the bacon to paper towels to drain. Spoon off all but 3 tablespoons of the drippings from the skillet.

Add the red onion and garlic to the drippings and cook, stirring often, until tender, 3–4 minutes. Add the salt, black pepper, thyme, and crushed red pepper and cook, stirring, for 30 seconds. Add the okra and toss to mix well with the onion and seasonings.

Add the tomatoes and bring to a boil. Reduce the heat to low, cover, and simmer, stirring occasionally, until the tomatoes and okra are tender, about 15 minutes. Sprinkle with the bacon, crumbling it coarsely, and the chives. Taste for seasoning. Serve hot.

# Ginger Tomatoes

*The first time I made this stunning dish, I used Black Plum toma-*
*toes, which grow like crazy in my garden. Upon retesting, I had only*
*the supermarket for tomato-picking. Happily, this recipe is lovely*
*even with out-of-season tomatoes, but choose small sweet ones, such*
*as Campari, or a mix of multicolored baby plums and large cherry*
*tomatoes. This is juicy, so serve it over freshly cooked white rice or*
*grits, and it would be excellent alongside sautéed shrimp. The dish*
*was inspired by a recipe in Nathalie Dupree's book* New Southern
Cooking. *A self-proclaimed ginger freak, Nathalie grows ginger,*
*along with benne seeds, lemongrass, Meyer lemons, and Kaffir*
*limes, in her Charleston, South Carolina, garden.*

MAKES 4 SIDE-DISH SERVINGS

---

2 tablespoons olive oil

1 garlic clove, minced

2 teaspoons peeled, finely chopped ginger

10–12 small, ripe, sweet tomatoes (1 pound), quartered or
   halved if very small (about 3 cups)

¼ teaspoon kosher salt

1½ teaspoons honey

2 tablespoons thinly sliced chives (garlic chives are great here)
   or scallion greens

---

Heat the olive oil in a large, heavy skillet over medium-high heat.
Add the garlic and ginger and cook, stirring, just until fragrant,
about 1 minute. Add the tomatoes, sprinkle with the salt, and
cook, tossing often, until they just start to collapse, 2–4 minutes.
Remove from the heat.

Add the honey, sprinkle with the chives or scallions, and mix
gently with a rubber spatula. The more you stir, the juicier they
get. Nathalie says to "dish them up hot."

# Simple Stewed Tomatoes

*This is not like what you get out of a can. Not even close. It's just tomatoes and onion cooked slowly in butter until rich, luscious, and sweet. The dish is based on thoughts from John Egerton and a recipe from* James Beard's American Cookery. *Customarily, stewed tomatoes have bread cubes added for thickening or sprinkled on top before they're served, and they're made with lots of sugar, but I held back so the tomatoes can shine true. Serve them in a bowl. Maybe crumble in some cornbread, or just serve this quintessential southern dish by itself.*

MAKES 4–6 SIDE-DISH SERVINGS

---

3 tablespoons unsalted butter
½ medium Vidalia onion, finely chopped (about 1 cup)
2–3 thyme sprigs
3 pounds ripe Amish Paste tomatoes, Romas, or sauce
    tomatoes, peeled, cored, and cut into chunks
    (about 6 cups)
1½ teaspoons kosher salt
1–2 teaspoons granulated sugar (optional)
½ teaspoon freshly ground black pepper

---

Melt the butter in a large, deep, heavy skillet or Dutch oven over medium heat. Add the onion and thyme sprigs and cook, stirring often, until tender, about 5 minutes. Add the tomatoes and bring to a boil. Reduce the heat, cover, and simmer until the tomatoes are soft and start to release their juices, about 15 minutes. Avoid the temptation to crush the tomatoes while they cook.

    Stir in the salt, sugar (if using), and pepper. Simmer, uncovered, over low heat, stirring occasionally, until the tomatoes are thickened a bit and very tender, 50–60 minutes. Discard the thyme sprigs. Taste for seasoning and serve hot.

# Savannah Red Rice

*My Savannah-born friend Margaret Shakespeare helped me perfect this Lowcountry specialty, a dish she loved at her grandmother's table. Baked in the oven, it yields separate, evenly infused, tomatoey grains of rice. Margaret liked the idea of adding toasted pecans to it and reminisced about the brown paper bags of fresh, shell-on pecans her granddaddy brought them from his South Carolina farm. Margaret, a writer, now lives in New York City. Since this recipe makes enough for a small crowd, she invited some of the ladies in her apartment building to supper. Canned tomatoes are the best choice here, giving a more tomato-rich flavor.*

MAKES 6–8 SIDE-DISH SERVINGS

---

1 28-ounce can whole tomatoes in juice
3 thick or 4 thin bacon slices, cut into ½-inch pieces
1½ cups finely chopped onion
1 cup coarsely chopped red bell pepper
1½ cups long-grain white rice
1 cup boiling reduced-sodium chicken broth
¼ cup tomato paste
1 teaspoon kosher salt
½ teaspoon dried thyme
¼ teaspoon freshly ground black pepper
⅛ teaspoon cayenne pepper
1 cup toasted and coarsely chopped pecans
   (optional but good)

---

Preheat the oven to 350°.

Pour the canned tomatoes into a colander set in a bowl. Press down lightly on each tomato to release the juice. Let drain for about 10 minutes, discarding the juice. Purée the tomatoes in a food processor until smooth (you should get about 1¾ cups).

Cook the bacon in a Dutch oven over medium heat, stirring often, until the fat is rendered, about 8 minutes. Add the onion and bell pepper and cook, stirring often, until tender, about 6 minutes.

Add the rice. Cook, stirring, reducing the heat if necessary, until the rice is coated and smells toasty, about 2 minutes. Add the puréed tomatoes, chicken broth, tomato paste, salt, thyme, and black and cayenne peppers. Stir well and bring to a boil. Boil for 1 minute and stir well again. Cover with a lid, transfer to the oven, and bake until the rice is just tender and the liquid has been absorbed, 35–40 minutes.

Remove from the oven and let stand, covered, for 5 minutes. Fluff well with a fork. Cover and let stand for another 5 minutes or until ready to serve. Taste for seasoning. Sprinkle with the pecans, if using, and serve hot.

# Sauces and Gravies

If you grow tomatoes or frequent a farmers' market, you know that when the season's juicy, colorful peak hits, you'll most likely have more fresh, ripe tomatoes than you have counter space in your kitchen or room on the porch, in the garage, or in the kids' rooms. Help is here! You can preserve summer's bounty deliciously with my End-of-Summer Big-Batch Tomato Sauce. Tuck it safely in the freezer so you can enjoy pasta dinners in the cooler months. There are also recipes for smaller-batch sauces, including a green tomato one and a Sungold sauce, plus Quick Rosemary Tomato Sauce, which becomes an easy weekday meal with canned tomatoes. And I've simmered up my version of an Appalachian Mountain tradition, tomato gravy. To further help you manage the harvest, there are easy how-to tips for freezing whole or cut-up tomatoes.

# End-of-Summer Big-Batch Tomato Sauce

*This is the sauce that I prepare in September and October with the baskets and bushels of tomatoes I harvest from my garden. I freeze it in zip-top bags that are stacked flat. When winter hits, I always know that a meal can be ready in the time it takes to cook pasta.*

*For a smooth texture, I run the cooked tomatoes through my food mill (page 99) before adding them to the flavor ingredients: the sautéed onions, peppers, garlic, and herbs. The food mill also removes any stray seeds or skins.*

MAKES ABOUT 15 CUPS

---

¼ cup plus 6 tablespoons olive oil, divided

10–12 pounds ripe tomatoes, at least half Amish Paste, San Marzano, or Romas and the rest assorted slicers or sauce tomatoes, peeled, cored, seeded, and cut into chunks (about 18 cups)

6–8 large garlic cloves, thinly sliced (about ⅓ cup)

1½ pounds assorted sweet peppers, such as Italian frying peppers, Cubanelles, and red bell peppers, halved, seeded, and cut in ½-inch pieces (about 5 cups)

2 medium Vidalia onions, coarsely chopped (about 4 cups)

2 teaspoons kosher salt, divided

1½ teaspoons dried oregano

1–1½ teaspoons crushed red pepper flakes (optional)

1 teaspoon fennel seed

½ teaspoon freshly ground black pepper

1 6-ounce can tomato paste, plus another ½ can if needed

1–2 cups chopped basil

---

Heat ¼ cup of the olive oil in a large, heavy Dutch oven over medium-high heat. Add the tomatoes and bring to a full boil, stirring often. Reduce the heat to medium-low. Simmer briskly, uncovered, stirring often and crushing the tomatoes with a potato masher, until very soft, about 20 minutes. Remove from the heat. Put through a food mill suspended over a narrow pot.

Rinse and dry the Dutch oven. Add the remaining 6 tablespoons olive oil and garlic. Cook over medium heat, stirring often, until the garlic just begins to brown at the edges, about 5 minutes. Add the peppers, onions, and 1 teaspoon of the salt. Cover and cook, stirring often, until the vegetables are very tender, 10–12 minutes. Stir in the oregano, crushed red pepper (if using), fennel, and black pepper; cook, stirring, for 1 minute.

Add the puréed tomatoes, tomato paste, and remaining 1 teaspoon salt. Mix well and bring to a boil. Reduce the heat to low and simmer, uncovered, stirring occasionally, for 15 minutes. Check the consistency. If not thick enough, add another half can of tomato paste. Simmer for 10–15 more minutes, until thickened and flavorful.

Stir in the basil and taste for seasoning. Cool completely before freezing. Ladle about 3 cups each into zip-top freezer bags or containers and seal. Label and date. Freeze for up to 8 months.

# Sungold Tomato Sauce

*Sungold cherry tomatoes, the tangerine-hued, juicy-sweet pops of flavor, are tops on everyone's list. They're also easy to grow, but be sure you have the space because the prolific plant can reach over six feet tall. My newspaper editor's young son, Jesse, loves them, and like a deer, he will eat a plant bare.*

*This sauce is on the thin side, so it is best tossed with a spoonable pasta, such as elbows or orzo, and served in bowls. Whole wheat pasta is especially good. Maybe cook some tiny peas or thin pieces of asparagus with the pasta for a minute before it's drained.*

MAKES 4–5 SERVINGS, ENOUGH FOR 1 POUND OF PASTA

3 tablespoons olive oil

3 large garlic cloves, minced

$\frac{1}{2}$ teaspoon dried oregano

$\frac{1}{2}$ teaspoon crushed red pepper flakes

4 cups halved Sungold cherry tomatoes

8 small, crisp yellow tomatoes, such as Yellow Perfection or yellow
   pear tomatoes (1 pound), halved or quartered (about 3 cups)

$\frac{3}{4}$ teaspoon kosher salt

$\frac{1}{4}$ cup chopped flat-leaf parsley

2 tablespoons chopped mint

Heat the olive oil in a large, deep, heavy skillet over medium-high heat. Add the garlic, oregano, and crushed red pepper and cook, stirring, until the garlic is fragrant, 2–3 minutes. Add the Sungold tomatoes, yellow tomatoes, and salt; bring to a boil. Reduce the heat slightly. Cook, stirring and mashing the tomatoes with a spoon, until they are very soft and have cooked down, about 10 minutes.

Put the sauce through a food mill suspended over a narrow pot or press it through a fine-mesh strainer, leaving only the skins and seeds behind. Reheat to serve, stir in the parsley and mint, and taste for seasoning.

## THE FOOD MILL

Generally, I'm pretty annoyed when a book tells me I need to buy something. So apologies. I used to think I didn't need a food mill either. But if you make large batches of tomato sauce or juice each year, you will want to get one.

Before I used a food mill, my tomato sauce contained stringy bits of tomato. The sauce can't be mashed sufficiently by hand, and the food processor made it too smooth. A food mill is what works.

Tomatoes are not difficult to pass through a food mill. It resembles a small saucepan with a perforated, conical base and a blade attached to a handle on top, secured on the underside by a nut. You anchor the food mill by the hooks on the sides over a narrow pot. Then put the tomatoes in the base and rotate the handle, both clockwise and counterclockwise, and the blade presses the tomato through the holes in the base. A thick tomato substance—the "good stuff"—clings to the underside, and you scrape it into the pot with a rubber spatula.

Wash it by hand and take care not to lose that nut. Mine is a Foley food mill. It's a tool you can pass on to your grandchildren, along with your recipes, of course.

# Quick Rosemary Tomato Sauce

*This is a recipe you'll turn to often in tomato season — or any-time — for a quick, delicious meal. Feel free to use any tomatoes that are getting soft or mealy. If you prefer a thicker sauce, stir in 1–2 tablespoons of tomato paste when it's nearly done. You can also make it with canned tomatoes.*

MAKES 4–5 SERVINGS, ENOUGH FOR 1 POUND OF PASTA

---

3 tablespoons olive oil

2 large garlic cloves, thinly sliced

2–3 rosemary sprigs (about 2 inches long)

3 pounds ripe tomatoes, about half San Marzanos or Romas
    and the rest heirlooms or sauce tomatoes, peeled, cored,
    and cut into rough ½-inch pieces (about 6 cups), or 2 28-
    ounce cans whole tomatoes in juice, drained (1 cup juice
    reserved), cut into ½-inch pieces

½ teaspoon kosher salt

¼ teaspoon freshly ground black pepper

---

Put the olive oil, garlic, and rosemary sprigs in a large, deep, heavy skillet over medium heat. Cook, stirring, until the garlic just starts to brown at the edges, about 3 minutes.

Add the fresh tomatoes (or the canned tomatoes and reserved juice), salt, and pepper and bring to a boil. Reduce the heat and simmer briskly, uncovered, stirring often and crushing the to-matoes with a potato masher, until the sauce is thickened and flavorful, 25–30 minutes. Remove the rosemary sprigs. (Some of the leaves will fall off, which I never mind.) Taste for seasoning.

## FREEZING TOMATOES

Whether you have a garden full of tomatoes or just a basket that you wish to put up, freezing is an easy, quick way to preserve the bounty. Or to keep it so it can be dealt with later. These methods work for big or small round tomatoes or Romas.

*Whole*: Select sound, unblemished tomatoes; rinse them well, brushing off any dirt, and pat dry. Pack into zip-top freezer bags, label, date, and freeze. To use, partially thaw at room temperature or in the fridge. While they're still quite icy, pull off the skins and cut or pull out the core. If you let them thaw completely, they'll melt into a puddle. You can also add them frozen and whole to stews, soups, or roasting vegetables, but you'll have to fish out the skins later as they often become tough. They'll keep for about 8 months.

*In pieces* (all prepped and recipe-ready): Peel, core, and cut into ½- to 1-inch pieces. Pack measured amounts (1 cup, 2 cups, etc.) in zip-top freezer bags or containers. Label with amount and date; freeze. No need to thaw before adding to most recipes, such as soups or stews. They'll keep for about 4 months.

*Prepared*: Tomato sauce, purées, some soups, and other preparations, generally those without cream, may be frozen in freezer containers or bags. Use within a few months, although tomato sauce will keep for at least 8 months.

# Abruzzo Green Tomato Pasta Sauce

*Green tomatoes are beloved in Italy, just as they are in the South, and not only for pasta. Italians, like southerners, enjoy tomatoes at all stages of ripeness. They also simmer green tomatoes for a jam that can be either sweet or savory and is served with meats, grilled polenta, or cake.*

*This special recipe comes by way of my* Pittsburgh Post-Gazette *colleague Gretchen McKay. It was given to Gretchen by her neighbor and good friend, Josephine Coletti, who is a native of the tiny town of Opi in the mountainous Abruzzi region of Italy. We like it best over a large pasta, like rigatoni, which has ridges to catch the chunky, tart sauce. Add lots of freshly grated Parmesan. This freezes well.*

MAKES 6 SERVINGS, ENOUGH FOR 1½ POUNDS OF PASTA

---

½ cup olive oil

6–8 large garlic cloves, minced (about ¼ cup)

2 tender medium celery stalks, chopped (about ¾ cup)

½ teaspoon crushed red pepper flakes, or more to taste

5–6 medium green tomatoes (2 pounds), cored and coarsely
   chopped (about 5 cups)

½ cup chopped flat-leaf parsley

1 teaspoon kosher salt

¼ teaspoon freshly ground black pepper

Pinch of baking soda

---

Put the olive oil and garlic in a large, heavy, deep skillet over medium heat. Cook, stirring, until fragrant, about 3 minutes. Add the celery and crushed red pepper and cook, stirring often, until tender, about 5 minutes. Add the green tomatoes, parsley, salt, and black pepper. Stir well and bring to a boil. Stir in the baking soda.

Reduce the heat to low, cover, and simmer, stirring occasionally and crushing the tomatoes with a potato masher, until they are very tender, about 25 minutes. For a thicker sauce, remove the cover and simmer about 5 more minutes. Taste for seasoning.

## THE POTATO MASHER

This tool could be renamed the *tomato* masher as often as I call for it in these pages. I love this low-tech, chord-free kitchen tool. It's great when you're making a sauce and you want it chunky, or mashing tomatoes for jam, or trying to make a soup more cohesive without resorting to a food processor or blender. It even works on potatoes.

Look for a potato masher with a stainless-steel masher and a wooden handle. It's a sturdy kitchen workhorse. You'll use it often.

# Tomato-Jalapeño Gravy

*The tradition of tomato gravy hails from the mountains and the hill counties of Appalachia. According to food writer Mark F. Sohn, tomato gravy, along with other flour-based gravies, is among the "great Appalachian foods."*

*It is not the Italian American Sunday gravy, simmered all day with cured and fresh meats and served over pasta. Tomato gravy is quickly made in a skillet, most often starting with drippings left from cooking bacon or side meat, which are then used to make a roux. Some add milk or cream in addition to tomatoes. I include a little jalapeño for zip.*

*Serve tomato gravy over biscuits, over rice, or on Fried Green Tomatoes (page 80) or sliced fresh ones. If you visit the Rising Creek Bakery and Café in Mount Morris, Pennsylvania, on the Pennsylvania–West Virginia line, you can have tomato gravy spooned over another Appalachian tradition: salt-rising bread.*

MAKES ABOUT 1 ¾ CUPS

---

4 thick bacon slices, cut into ¾-inch pieces

1 medium onion, chopped (about ½ cup)

1 jalapeño pepper, minced, with some or all of the seeds

2 tablespoons plus 1½ teaspoons all-purpose flour

3–4 large, ripe, juicy tomatoes such as Mountain Princess, West Virginia, Oxheart, or Celebrity (1½ pounds), grated (about 2 cups)

¾ cup reduced-sodium chicken broth

¼ teaspoon kosher salt

¼ teaspoon freshly ground black pepper

---

Cook the bacon in a large, heavy skillet (not cast-iron) over medium heat, stirring often, until it is crisp and the fat is rendered, about 8 minutes. With a slotted spoon, transfer to paper towels to drain (add to the gravy later or reserve for another dish). Spoon off all but 3 tablespoons of the drippings from the skillet.

Add the onion and jalapeño to the drippings. Reduce the heat to low. Cook, stirring often, until tender, 3–4 minutes. Stir in the flour and cook, stirring, until flecked medium-brown, about 2 minutes.

Stir in the tomatoes and chicken broth. Increase the heat and bring to a boil, stirring from the bottom of the skillet to incorporate the roux. Reduce the heat to very low and simmer, uncovered, stirring often (this gravy likes to stick), until it has thickened and the flavors are blended, 20–25 minutes.

Stir in the salt and pepper and add the bacon, if you like, crumbling it coarsely. Taste again, making sure there is enough pepper. Serve hot.

# Desserts

Tomatoes for dessert? Let me tempt you.

Tomatoes are botanically fruits—specifically, berries. That is, they start out as flowers and turn into fruits, containing the seeds of the plant. While tomatoes are most often used as vegetables and treated in savory ways, in this chapter, we turn things around.

Most tomatoes are not sweet by themselves, but they do marry well with sweet things, such as sugar, sorghum syrup, and honey, and they love aromatics, like cinnamon, nutmeg, and ginger. They also come alive when paired with other fruits, such as apples and raisins. So either baked in a crust or stirred in a batter with bourbon and brown sugar, tomatoes can be sweetly transformed into dessert. Dig in; these recipes are delicious.

# Spiced Green Tomato Crumb Cake

*Boozy raisins, warm spices, and a pecan-crumb topping star in this cake. The green tomatoes add texture, moisture, and a bit of whimsy. Use the precise amount of them; the weight and cup measures are your guides. This cake freezes beautifully.*

MAKES 12 OR MORE SERVINGS

**FOR THE TOPPING**

½ cup granulated sugar

⅓ cup all-purpose flour

½ teaspoon cinnamon

½ teaspoon ground ginger

½ cup chopped pecans

4 tablespoons unsalted butter, at room temperature

**FOR THE CAKE**

½ cup golden raisins, soaked in ¼ cup bourbon or Jack Daniels

2–3 medium, firm green tomatoes (14 ounces), cored, pared with a vegetable peeler, and cut into ½-inch pieces (2½ cups)

2¼ cups all-purpose flour

2 teaspoons baking powder

½ teaspoon baking soda

1½ teaspoons cinnamon

1 teaspoon ground ginger

½ teaspoon fine table salt

1 stick unsalted butter, at room temperature

¾ cup granulated sugar

½ cup packed dark brown sugar

2 large eggs, at room temperature

1 teaspoon vanilla extract

½ cup buttermilk or plain yogurt (don't use Greek yogurt)

Preheat the oven to 350°. Butter a 13 × 9-inch glass baking dish.

To make the topping, stir together the sugar, flour, cinnamon, and ginger in a medium bowl. Add the pecans and butter and mix with your fingers or a fork until crumbly. Set the topping aside.

To make the cake, soak the raisins in the bourbon for about 30 minutes. Put the green tomatoes in a colander and place in the sink to drain until needed. Stir together the flour, baking powder, baking soda, cinnamon, ginger, and salt in a large bowl.

Beat the butter with an electric mixer on medium speed in another large bowl until creamy. Add the sugars and beat until light and fluffy. Scrape the bowl. Add the eggs, one at a time, beating well after each addition. Beat in the vanilla; scrape the bowl. With the mixer on low, add the dry ingredients in 3 additions, alternating with the buttermilk or yogurt, just until mixed.

By hand, fold in the drained green tomatoes and the raisins with any unabsorbed bourbon. Scrape the batter into the prepared pan. Sprinkle evenly with the topping.

Bake until the cake is browned and springy to the touch and a toothpick inserted in the center comes out clean, 40–45 minutes. Transfer to a wire rack and serve the cake warm or at room temperature.

# Green Tomato and Apple Pie

*Green tomato pies are an old and wonderful tradition in southern cooking. According to Nancie McDermott, author of* Southern Pies: A Gracious Plenty of Pie Recipes, from Lemon Chess to Chocolate Pecan, *green tomato pie is based on apple pie. "Double crust, the usual spices, flour and butter to thicken it a bit. It's a way to make use of end-of-season tomatoes, and a way to sweeten the table. In the spirit of letting nothing go to waste."*

*Breaking with tradition just a little, I added some fresh apple to my pie. The textures and flavors contrast and complement each other beautifully.*

MAKES 6–8 SERVINGS

---

Pastry for a 9-inch double-crust pie (can be store-bought)

4–5 medium, firm green tomatoes (1½ pounds), pared with a
    vegetable peeler, halved, cored, and cut into ¼-inch-thick
    wedges (about 4 cups)

1 cup granulated sugar

¼ cup plus 2 tablespoons all-purpose flour

1 teaspoon cinnamon

¼ teaspoon nutmeg

¼ teaspoon fine table salt

2 medium, sweet-tart apples, such as Golden Delicious or
    Gala (12 ounces), peeled, cored, and cut into ¼-inch-thick
    slices (about 2 cups)

1 tablespoon lemon juice

2 tablespoons unsalted butter, cut up

2 tablespoons packed light brown sugar

2 teaspoons cream or whole milk

Topping: 1 tablespoon granulated sugar mixed with
    ¼ teaspoon cinnamon

---

Preheat the oven to 425°. Fit one piece of pastry into a 9-inch pie plate, trimming the overhanging edges to about 1 inch. Refrigerate while preparing the filling.

Spread the green tomatoes on a double layer of paper towels and let drain for about 5 minutes. Blot dry.

Stir together the granulated sugar, flour, cinnamon, nutmeg, and salt in a large bowl. Add the apples and green tomatoes and drizzle with the lemon juice. Toss to mix well. Pile into the pie plate. Dot with the butter; sprinkle with the brown sugar.

Moisten the edge of the bottom pastry with water. Fit the other piece of pastry over the filling, pressing the edges together and trimming, if necessary. Flute the edge or crimp it with a floured fork. Cut three slits in the top of the pastry to allow steam to escape. Brush with the cream or milk and sprinkle with the cinnamon-sugar topping.

Place the pie plate on a baking sheet. Bake in the lower third of the oven for 15 minutes. Reduce the oven temperature to 375°. Bake until the juices are bubbly and thickened and the fruit is tender, 45–50 more minutes. Carefully remove the pie from the baking sheet to a wire rack and cool completely.

# Preserves and Juices

Taking the idea of treating tomatoes as fruit several steps further, here you'll find tomato jam, chutney, and conserve, sweet and spicy, thick and addictive, to spread on biscuits or serve with cheese or roasted meats. I've also included a family favorite, Green Tomato Bread-and-Butter Pickles, which are great right from the jar and even better as an accompaniment to cured and smoked meats. Last, making your own tomato juice is the ultimate way of preserving the harvest, and you can use this final recipe in the book to make a terrific rendition of the first recipe, the Bloody Mary. Tomatoes come full circle.

# Heirloom Tomato Jam with Lemon

*This jam is fabulous—crimson-hued and just sweet enough, with the tart kiss of lemon. It makes a wonderful harvest gift. If you wish to, you can process it in a boiling-water canner for 15 minutes. Start timing after the water returns to a boil. Use big flavor-packed heirlooms here. The recipe was inspired by one in Sharon Nimtz and Ruth Cousineau's* Tomato Imperative! *Tomato jams, marmalades, and conserves are a very old and delightful concept.*

MAKES 3–4 HALF-PINT JARS

---

4 pounds ripe heirloom tomatoes, such as Cherokee Purple, Brandywine, or Delicious, including an Amish Paste or a few Romas, peeled, cored, seeded, and cut into ½-inch pieces (about 5½ cups)

1 medium lemon, preferably organic, halved lengthwise and thinly sliced crosswise, seeds removed

2½ cups granulated sugar

3–5 tablespoons lemon juice

---

Put the tomatoes and lemon slices in a large, heavy, deep skillet or Dutch oven over medium-high heat. Stir well and bring to a boil, crushing the tomatoes with a potato masher. Simmer for 10 minutes.

Stir in the sugar, reduce the heat to medium, and simmer, uncovered, stirring frequently and skimming off any foam, until thick, about 30 minutes. Stir in 3 tablespoons lemon juice and cook until thickened and jamlike, 5–8 more minutes. Taste, and if it's too sweet, add 1–2 tablespoons more lemon juice and return to a full boil.

Spoon immediately into clean, hot, half-pint jars and fit the jars with 2-piece lids. Let cool, then refrigerate the jam until ready to serve.

## JAMMIN'

To test whether a jam or preserve is ready, chill a small plate in the freezer. Drop a spoonful of the preserves onto the plate, then place it back in the freezer for a few minutes, until cooled but not chilled. If the preserves are set and remain in a mound, without running, they're ready.

Another method is called the sheeting test. Dip a metal spoon into the preserves and scoop up a spoonful. Hold it over a plate and watch to see if the preserves drop off the spoon in what resembles sheets or flakes, meaning they are ready. You'll get more familiar with this over time.

# Tomato and Golden Raisin Chutney

*This chutney is not too sweet, has deep spicy notes, and is very nice with cheese and whole-grain crackers, on grilled pork chops, or with salmon. The tomatoes are not seeded here. I did not process it, though you could do so in a boiling-water canner for 10 minutes.*

MAKES 3–4 HALF-PINT JARS

---

3 pounds firm-but-ripe, meaty tomatoes, such as Oxheart or
    Amish Paste, peeled, cored, and cut into ½-inch pieces
    (about 6 cups)

1 pound baby yellow or red pear tomatoes, Juliet tomatoes,
    or Sungold cherry tomatoes, not peeled, halved if large
    (about 2½ cups)

¾ cup golden raisins

1 cup cider vinegar

1 cup granulated sugar

½ cup packed light brown sugar

3 tablespoons peeled, finely grated ginger

3 garlic cloves, minced

2 teaspoons kosher salt

¾ teaspoon cayenne pepper

½ teaspoon turmeric

---

Put the large tomatoes, small tomatoes, raisins, vinegar, sugars, ginger, garlic, salt, cayenne pepper, and turmeric in a heavy Dutch oven. Mix well and bring to a boil over medium-high heat, stirring to dissolve the sugars.

Reduce the heat to medium-low so that the chutney is simmering briskly. Cook, uncovered, stirring occasionally, skimming off any foam, and crushing large chunks with a potato masher. Reduce the heat as it starts to thicken. Continue simmering the chutney until it is very thick and jamlike, about 1 hour and 45 minutes.

Spoon the chutney immediately into clean, hot, half-pint jars and fit the jars with 2-piece lids. Let cool, then refrigerate until ready to serve.

# Green Tomato
# Bread-and-Butter Pickles

*My father loves these pickles, and he especially enjoyed them with a pastrami sandwich we once brought him on a visit. I think he liked the pickles better than the pastrami, so I gave him another jar and now have a mandate for next year. Gently scrub the tomatoes first with a soft brush and rinse thoroughly. Since they're not peeled, any dirt that adheres could cause the pickles to spoil. These are processed in a boiling-water canner for longer storage.*

MAKES 7–8 HALF-PINT JARS

9–10 medium, firm green tomatoes (3 pounds), cored and cut crosswise into 1/4-inch-thick slices, ends discarded (about 9 cups)

1/4 cup kosher salt

2 1/2 cups cider vinegar

1 1/4 cups granulated sugar

1/2 cup packed light brown sugar

1 tablespoon mustard seeds

1 1/2 teaspoons ground ginger

1 teaspoon turmeric

1 teaspoon freshly ground black pepper

1/2 teaspoon whole allspice berries, coarsely crushed with a mortar and pestle

1/2 teaspoon celery seeds

3 medium onions, halved and thinly sliced (about 2 cups)

7–8 small fresh or dried hot peppers (optional)

Layer the green tomatoes and salt in a large glass bowl or a ceramic crock. Cover with plastic wrap and let stand at room temperature for 12 hours or overnight. Transfer to a large colander and drain well, but don't rinse or press down on the slices.

Stir together the vinegar, sugars, mustard seeds, ginger, turmeric, pepper, allspice, and celery seeds in a Dutch oven over high heat. Bring to a boil, stirring to dissolve the sugars. Stir in the onions. Reduce the heat, cover, and simmer for 5 minutes. Stir in the green tomatoes and return to a boil. Cover and simmer, stirring occasionally, for 5 more minutes.

Pack the tomatoes, onions, and syrup into clean, hot, half-pint jars, leaving a ¼-inch headspace. Add a hot pepper to each, if you like. Fit the jars with 2-piece lids. Process in a boiling-water canner for 10 minutes. Begin timing after the water has returned to a boil. Store for at least 2 weeks in a dark, cool place before opening.

## CANNING TIPS

The most frequent advice I give on home canning is "get thee a copy of *The Ball Blue Book Guide to Preserving*." It's the preserving bible, with all the information you need.

Grandmother's recipes may be prized, but some of her canning methods are no longer considered safe. Low-acid foods, such as green beans, which are not packed in an acidic medium of vinegar or in pickling brine, must be processed in a pressure-canner. On the other hand, dilly beans or my Green Tomato Bread-and-Butter Pickles are high-acid because they are packed in a solution of sugar, vinegar, and salt, and they can be safely processed in a boiling-water canner.

Packing hot cooked foods into a jar and just tightening the lid or turning the jar over to heat the sealing compound on the lid in lieu of water-bath processing is also considered unsafe. While the jar may initially seal, a vacuum has not been created inside it. The lid could unseal later, and the food could spoil. Any pickle and preserve recipes in this book that are not processed, once cooled, must be stored in the refrigerator.

Tomatoes, which you might think of as an acidic food, need additional acid for safe canning, according to the USDA. You must add 2 tablespoons *bottled* (not fresh) lemon juice to each quart jar of tomatoes and 1 tablespoon to each pint jar in order to reach the proper acidity.

# Red Tomato and Jalapeño
# Conserve, for Nathalie

*I made this for Nathalie Dupree, a terrific food writer and a gener-
ous friend. She doesn't care for the concept of a sweet tomato jam.
She makes her tomato jam with vinegar and sugar, as her mother-
in-law did, and calls it a conserve. Nathalie adores it spooned atop
pole beans and butterbeans.*

*I think both my sweet Heirloom Tomato Jam with Lemon and
this conserve have a place in tomato history. But this is the one
Nathalie likes best. This is not processed, though you could process
it in a boiling-water canner for 10 minutes. You could also leave
out the jalapeño, but I love the little bite.*

MAKES 5–6 HALF-PINT JARS

---

5 pounds firm-but-ripe, meaty tomatoes, such as Arkansas
   Traveler, Amish Paste, or Celebrity, peeled, cored, seeded,
   and cut into chunks (about 7 heaping cups)
4–5 jalapeño peppers, minced, with some or all of the seeds
1¼ cups cider vinegar
1½ cups granulated sugar
⅓ cup packed light brown sugar
1½ teaspoons kosher salt

---

Put the tomatoes, jalapeños, vinegar, sugars, and salt in a heavy
Dutch oven. Mix well and bring to a boil over high heat, stirring
to dissolve the sugar.

Reduce the heat to medium-low so that the conserve is simmering briskly. Cook, uncovered, stirring occasionally, skimming
off any foam, and crushing large chunks with a potato masher.
Reduce the heat as it starts to thicken. Continue simmering the
conserve until it is very thick and jamlike, about 1 hour and
30 minutes to 1 hour and 45 minutes. Spoon immediately into
clean, hot, half-pint jars and fit the jars with 2-piece lids. Let
cool, then refrigerate until ready to serve.

# Fresh-Brewed Tomato Juice

*This tastes nothing like the commercial stuff. Use smaller, intensely flavorful tomatoes in this recipe; save the big, beefy guys for salads and sandwiches. If you want to can the juice, to reach the proper acidity, add 2 tablespoons bottled (not fresh) lemon juice to each quart. Processing time in a boiling-water canner is 40 minutes for pints, 45 minutes for quarts. Lemon juice alters the flavor, so I like to make a batch to use right away and maybe can some for later. Scrub the tomatoes first with a soft brush and rinse them well, cutting away any bruises or blemishes before you begin.*

MAKES ABOUT 1 QUART

---

3 pounds small ripe tomatoes, cored and quartered
1½ teaspoons kosher salt
½–1 teaspoon granulated sugar (optional)

---

Put the tomatoes in a Dutch oven over medium heat. Cook, stirring often and crushing the tomatoes with a potato masher, until they begin to release their juices and boil.

Reduce the heat to medium-low, cover, and simmer, stirring occasionally and crushing the tomatoes, until they are very soft and all the juices have been released, 15–17 minutes. Put through a food mill suspended over a narrow pot or press through a fine-mesh strainer, leaving only the seeds and skins behind. Stir in the salt and sugar, if desired, to taste.

Transfer to a jar or other container and let cool. Cover and chill until ready to serve.

# Acknowledgments

I would like to thank Elaine Maisner and the University of North Carolina Press for letting me write about the vegetable (fruit) I love the best. Thanks to Gina Mahalek for her friendship, to Paula Wald for her patience and skill, and to the entire team at UNC Press for their good work. I am grateful to Marcie Cohen Ferris and William Ferris for their encouragement and friendship. For invaluable editing assistance and for always giving me a break and a forum, many thanks to Bob Batz Jr., top comma-buster and my editor at the *Pittsburgh Post-Gazette*, where I write my column, "Miriam's Garden."

The introduction was enhanced by Andrew F. Smith's scholarship on tomatoes. Thanks also to Barbara Melera of D. Landreth Seed Company, who shared her expertise on the Trophy Tomato and early tomato history. I am also indebted to Damon Lee Fowler, who patiently answered my questions.

For assistance with recipes, hugs to Margaret Shakespeare, China Millman, and Terry Feingold. Because no one could ever grow as many tomatoes as I needed, thanks much to Jeanne Williams and Wendy Saul. I am grateful to Sheri Castle for sharing her recipe. For assistance with being southern, thanks to Sheri, Fred Thompson and Belinda Ellis, Nathalie Dupree, Nancie McDermott, and Virginia Willis. For always answering questions and sharing stories, thanks to Carroll Leggett.

Gratitude to my friends Jennifer McLagan, Linda Cedarbaum, and Marie Simmons for believing in me. To my mother, Dianne Rubin, for teaching me to love gardening, and my father, Irving Rubin, for teaching me to love food. And to friends whom we missed during the summer I was writing this. Come this year. We'll eat tomatoes!

The patience award goes to my husband, David Lesako, who tells me every year that I can't plant more tomatoes than we have cages for but has never told me how many cages we have.

# Bibliography

Algood, Tammy. *The Complete Southern Cookbook*. Philadelphia: Running Press, 2010.

Bailey, Lee. *Lee Bailey's Tomatoes*. New York: Clarkson Potter, 1992.

Bailey, Liberty Hyde. *The Survival of the Unlike: A Collection of Evolution Essays Suggested by the Study of Domestic Plants*. New York: Macmillan, 1896.

Baker Creek Heirloom Seeds. 2012 Seed Book. www.rareseeds.com.

Beard, James. *James Beard's American Cookery*. Boston: Little, Brown, 1972.

Bryan, Mrs. Lettice. *The Kentucky Housewife*. Cincinnati: Shepard and Stearns, 1839.

Council, Mildred. *Mama Dip's Kitchen*. Chapel Hill: University of North Carolina Press, 1999.

D. Landreth Seed Company. Catalog. www.landrethseeds.com.

Davidson, Alan. *The Oxford Companion to Food*. Oxford: Oxford University Press, 1999.

Dull, Mrs. S. R. *Southern Cooking*. 1928. Reprint, Athens: University of Georgia Press, 2006.

Dupree, Nathalie. *New Southern Cooking*. New York: Knopf, 1986.

Edge, John T., ed. *Foodways*. Vol. 7 of *The New Encyclopedia of Southern Culture*. Chapel Hill: University of North Carolina Press, 2007.

Egerton, John (with Ann Egerton). *Southern Food: At Home, on the Road, in History*. New York: Knopf, 1987.

Ferris, Marcie Cohen. *Matzoh Ball Gumbo: Culinary Tales of the Jewish South*. Chapel Hill: University of North Carolina Press, 2005.

Fowler, Damon Lee. *Classical Southern Cooking*. Salt Lake City: Gibbs Smith, 2008.

Glenn, Camille. *The Heritage of Southern Cooking*. New York: Workman, 1986.

Hill, Mrs. Annabella P. *Mrs. Hill's New Cook Book*. New York: James O'Kane, 1867.

Jordan, Michele Anna. *The Good Cook's Book of Tomatoes*. Reading: Addison-Wesley, 1995.

Junior Auxiliary of Vicksburg, Mississippi. *Vintage Vicksburg.*
Memphis: Wimmer Cookbooks, 1985.

Ladies of the Presbyterian Church, Paris, Ky., eds. *Housekeeping in the Blue Grass: A New and Practical Cook Book.* Cincinnati: Geo. E. Stevens & Co., 1875.

Lewis, Edna. *The Taste of Country Cooking.* New York: Knopf, 1976.

Lewis, Edna, and Scott Peacock. *The Gift of Southern Cooking: Recipes and Revelations from Two Great American Cooks.* New York: Knopf, 2003.

Lundy, Ronni. *In Praise of Tomatoes: Tasty Recipes, Garden Secrets, Legends and Lore.* New York: Lark Books, 2004.

Male, Carolyn J. *100 Heirloom Tomatoes for the American Garden.* New York: Workman, 1999.

Mann, Charles C. *1493: Uncovering the New World Columbus Created.* New York: Knopf, 2011.

Marks, Gil. *The Encyclopedia of Jewish Food.* Hoboken: Wiley, 2010.

McDermott, Nancie. *Southern Pies: A Gracious Plenty of Pie Recipes, from Lemon Chess to Chocolate Pecan.* San Francisco: Chronicle Books, 2010.

Metcalfe, Gayden, and Charlotte Hays. *Being Dead Is No Excuse: The Official Southern Ladies Guide to Hosting the Perfect Funeral.* New York: Miramax, 2005.

National Gardening Association. *Dictionary of Horticulture.* New York: Penguin, 1994.

Nimtz, Sharon, and Ruth Cousineau. *Tomato Imperative!: From Fried Green Tomatoes to Summer's Ripe Bounty.* New York: Little, Brown, 1994.

*Old-Fashioned Tomato Recipes.* Indianapolis, Ind.: Bear Wallow Press, 1981.

Randolph, Mrs. Mary. *The Virginia Housewife or Methodical Cook.* Philadelphia: Butler, 1824.

Smith, Andrew F. "Authentic Fried Green Tomatoes?" *Food History News* 4 (Summer 1992): 1–2.

———. *Souper Tomatoes: The Story of America's Favorite Food.* New Brunswick, N.J.: Rutgers University Press, 2000.

———. *The Tomato in America: Early History, Culture, and Cookery.* Urbana: University of Illinois Press, 1994.

Southern Exposure Seed Catalogue. Catalogue and Garden Guide, 2011. www.southernexposure.com.

Villas, James. *The Glory of Southern Cooking*. Hoboken: Wiley, 2007.
Watson, Benjamin. *Taylor's Guide to Heirloom Vegetables*. Boston: Houghton Mifflin, 1996.
Weaver, William Woys. *Heirloom Vegetable Gardening: A Master Gardener's Guide to Planting, Seed Saving, and Cultural History*. New York: Henry Holt, 1997.

# Index